MAHARANA RAJ SINGH AND HIS TIMES

Other works on History by Sri Ram Sharma

Bibliography of Mughal India
Religious Policy of the Mughal Emperors
Mughal Government and Administration
Maharana Pratap
Studies in Medieval Indian History
A Dutch Chronicle of Mughal India (with Prof. Brij Narain)
Constitutional History of India
Evolution of Public Administration in India (a source book)
From Buddha to Harsha (a source book), (in the press)
An outline of Indian History
India in Ferment
Mahatma Hansraj, a Maker of Modern Punjab.

Maharana Raj Singh and His Times

Sri Ram Sharma
Director, Institute of Public Administration
UNA

MOTILAL BANARSIDASS
DELHI :: PATNA :: VARANASI

Head Office : BUNGALOW ROAD, JAWAHAR NAGAR, DELHI-7
Branches : (1) CHOWK, VARANASI-1 (U.P.)
(2) ASHOK RAJPATH, PATNA-4 (BIHAR)

First Edition
1971
Price

PRINTED IN INDIA BY SHANTILAL JAIN AT SHRI JAINENDRA PRESS, BUNGALOW ROAD, JAWAHAR NAGAR, DELHI-7, AND PUBLISHED BY SUNDARLAL JAIN, MOTILAL BANARSIDASS, BUNGALOW ROAD, JAWAHAR NAGAR, DELHI-7

PREFACE

The following pages make an attempt at studying a period of history of Marwar when it was inextricably mixed up with the general history of India. The last sack of Chitor under Shahjahan, Aurangzeb's rebellion against his father Shahjahan, death of Jaswant Singh of Jodhpur and the attempt of Aurangzeb to incorporate it into imperial domains, the resultant war in Rajputana where for the first time after the battle of Khanua, a century and a half earlier, many Rajput clans fought shoulder to shoulder against Mughals are as much a part of the general history of India as of that of Mewar.

In going over a much trodden ground my only excuse is that this is the first comprehensive attempt to cover the field on the basis of all the material accessible to us today in many languages—Persian, Sanskrit, Hindi and English. For another thing the sources used include not only the contemporary or semi-contemporary histories but official records and inscriptions as well. Full critical use has been made for the first time of the *Rājapraśasti Mahākāvyam* of Ranchhod Bhat and *Rāj Vilās* of Mān. The official records in Mewar Archives as reproduced in the *Vīr Vinod* have also been examined along with Mughal records of the same events to yield a coherent story. The minutes of the Emperors' court as preserved in the contemporary Akhabārāt (News-Letters) and *Jaipur Records*, Prince Akbar's Despatches from the scene of battle in 1680 preserved in the *Ādāb-i-Ālamgīrī*, Chandar Bhan's account of his mission to Udaipur, and correspondence between various actors in and onlookers of the contemporary scene afford a more comprehensive view thereof than is possible in many other fields of medieval Indian History.

For another thing the *Rājapraśasti Mahākāvyam* and *Rāj Vilās* offer us a picture of certain religious and social customs such as is not available elsewhere. The former resembles in part a chief engineer's report read at the inauguration ceremony of the great dam constituting the Rajsamund lake and in part a publicity campaign after the ceremony was over.

As the following pages would reveal I have approached all my sources with a view to understand the events they try to describe. I have no bias in favour of or against sources in any language or in any medium as such. I have found that it is no more difficult to make a misstatement in a writing on paper as in an inscription on stone and almost as easy to conceal the true nature of an event in Persian as in Hindi or Sanskrit. I further found that here, as elsewhere, it is not necessary to assume that official account of an event issued in the heat of the moment was any the more trustworthy in the past than it is today. The reports of the news-writers in the province of Ajmer for the turbulent years 1679—1680 seem to be as reliable as the reports of the C.I.D. in the Punjab during 1907—1910 when the province was in ferment. I have therefore been content to tell my story as it has emerged after a critical examination of the source material.

To my predecessor in the field, particularly James Tod, Kaviraj Shyamal Dar, Sir Jodunath Sarkar, Pandit Gaurishankar Ojha, Munshi Devi Prasad I am indebted for the insight their labours afforded me. Shri N.P. Chakravarti and Dr. B.C. Chabra's edition of the Rajapraśasti has been of an immense help for which I am thankful to them both. I am grateful to Lala Jagan Nath Aggarwal, head of the Vishveshvaranand Institute of Indian Culture, for his valuable help in translating the Sanskrit extracts into English.

I am thankful to Dr Khaliq Ahmad Nizami, Professor of History, Muslim University, Aligarh, for his help in securing the manuscript of Chander Bhan's account of the conquest of Chitor from MSS. in the University Library, Aligarh.

I am thankful to Pandit Bhagat Ram Shastri for his help in reading the proofs.

Sri Ram Sharma

CONTENTS

Chapter I

THE RĀJAPRAŚSTI MAHĀKĀVYAM

The practice of damming a stream to create an artificial lake seems to go back at least to the sixteenth century in India. Rana Udai singh of Mewar is said to have planned a dam near Raj Nagar but given up this plan in favour of a less ambitious and less expensive project of creating the Udai Sagar lake near Udaipur. Rana Raj Singh (1653 to 1680) while on his journey to Jaisalmer to marry a Bhatti princess in 1698 A. V. (1641 A.D.) is said to have conceived the idea of building a dam near Raj Nagar[1]. Raj Singh was only twelve then. It is not likely that such an ambitious project could have been thought of by him at such a tender age.

But when as a reigning monarch he was on a pilgrimage to the Rūpanārāyaṇa temple at Sevantri near Kankaroli, he passed through the same countryside and halted at Dhodhunda, he decided to build a dam across the Gomati[2], damming the waters of the Talá and the Kailana as well into an artificial lake[2]. Mān tells us that the building of the dam followed three years of draught. For want of water the world was in despair and people went mad with hunger. Things unknown as food were eaten. The husband abandoned the wife, the wife the husband; parents sold their children. Time increased the evil, it spread far and wide. Those who got something to eat today, ate twice what nature required...... ....Rivers, lakes, fountains dried up. Men of wealth meted out the portions of food...There was no longer any distinction of caste, and the Shudra and the Brahmans were undistinguishable..Fruits, flowers, every vegetable thing, even trees were stripped of their bark to apease the pangs of hunger. Cities were depopulated. The seed of families was lost, fish became extinct and the hope of all was extinguished[3].

1. Ranchhod, Canto IX, Verses 2 to 7.
2. Ibid, IX, 9 and 10.
3. Mān, VIII, 136 to 139.

Another tradition would have it that the dam was built as an act of expiation. Maharana Raj Singh is said to have caused the death of Udai Ram Bhatta, Kanwar Sultan Singh, a Purohita, one of his Ranis and Kanwar Sardar Singh. He is said to have been advised that he could expiate for his sins by causing a great tank to be built[4]. The work began in 1660 A. D. (1717 A. V.) and was completed in 1678 A.D. (1735 A.V.). This was named Rajasamund.

Fortunately for us a record of the building of the dam, its dedication and the ceremonies performed when it was consecrated has come down to us in the *Rājapraśasti*, a contemporary work in verse consisting of 24 cantos of the main narrative and an invocatory additional canto. The preserved text is incised on 25 marble slabs; 24 fixed in the walls of the Nauchauki Ghat of the Rajasamund and one inside a pavilion on the same Ghat.

The author of this 'Mahākāvya' describes himself as Ranchhod Bhatt, son of Madhusudan Bhatt, a Telangana Brahman of Kothondi *Kula.* His mother was Veni, a daughter of Gosvami Yadunath[5]. The family seems to have frequently received gifts from Rana Raj Singh and his father Jagat Singh[6]. The author, either for want of anything else to lengthen out his narrative or anxious lest his readers should forget whose work they are studying, repeats his genealogy with more or less variations frequently at the end of many of the cantos.

If we were to believe our author, his father occupied a very important place in Raj Singh's court as a diplomat.

In 1653 Shahjahan sent 30,000 horse under the command of Saadullah Khan, his prime minister, against Mewar. After Saadullah Khan had occupied Chitor and demolished the additions to and repairs of the fort, our author asserts, Raj Singh sent Madhusudan as an envoy to Saadullah Khan[7]. We know from other contemporary records, including the memoirs of one of the chief participants in the negotiations,

4. *Vir Vinod,* II, 446.
5. Ranchhod, I, 30, 31.
6. Ibid, V, 33, 43, 45, 46, 50, VI, 27, 28, 38, 39, 41, 42, 45, 46.
7. Ibid, VI, 12, 13.

Chandar Bhan, that the Mewar mission was composed of Ram Chand Chauhan, Ragho Das Jhala, Sanval Dass Rathor and Purohita Gharib Dass[8]. Madhusudan is not mentioned at all by these writers. But still more surprising is the author's account of the negotiations. They might read as good repartee, but the saucy answers to Saadullah Khan's complaints, which we know from other records Raj Singh had to admit as true[9] could not have turned away Shahjahan's wrath. It is interesting to record that our author was so flattered at Saadullah Khan's calling Madhusudan a 'Pandit', that he included the fact in the record with pride[10]. Madhusudan could not have been the spokesman of the Mewar mission though he may have been one of the party.

It is rather curious to note that Purohita Gharib Das had a son named Ranchhod. We may very well ask ourselves if the work of the father of one Ranchhod has been assigned to the father of another Ranchhod or is Gharib Dass another name of Madhusudan Pandit? The first possibility may raise difficult problems about our author's probity but only where his own family is concerned, Gharib Das and his son Ranchhod, it may be noted, occupied such a high position at court that the father had himself weighed against gold and the son against silver when the consecration ceremony of the Rajasamund took place[11]. Ranchhod, son of Gharib Dass, laid the foundation of the dam on 17 th April, 1665[12]. Gharib Dass and Ranchhod are again mentioned as being present along with Raj Singh, his sons and grandsons, his brother, other princes and the prime minister in the pavilion erected for the performance of the ceremonies connected with the consecration of the lake[13]. The only service which our author records himself as performing on the occasion of the consecration is to carry gifts to Raja Jaswant Singh Rathor of Jodhpur[14].

8. Chandar Bhan, *Chahar Chaman*, IV; *Inshai Brahman*,
9. Chandar Bhan, *Chahar Chaman*, IV, *Inshai Brahman*.
10. Ranchhod VI, 14 to 28.
11. Ibid, XVIII, 10, 11.
12. Ibid, IX, 37.
13. Ibid XIV 20, XVII, 5.
14. Ibid, XX, 1 to 4

Of course Madusudan and his family figure elsewhere in the record as recipients of gifts from Jagat Singh and Raj Singh. Thirty 'Umā-maheśvara' gifts were made to Madhusudan and his wife, Veni, by various princes of the Mewar house[15]. It is amusing to note that after the completion of Madhusudan's alleged diplomatic mission to Saadullah Khan, he was fobbed off with a payment of Rs 500 in place of an elephant[16]. Similarly we are told that Raj Singh claimed the merit of performing the horse sacrifice by giving to Madhusudan a white horse adorned with a gold saddle (?) in 1657[17]. Madhusudan is said to have accompanied Raj Singh during his pilgrimage to and stay at Banaras[18].

Ranchhod tells us that he was asked to compose the present work by Raj Singh[19] on January 1, 1662 on the day the order to commence the construction of the dam was issued[20]. The Mahākāvya is said to have been completed on Magha Purnima in 1732 A.V. (20th January 1676) on the day the consecration of the lake took place[21]. This obviously cannot be true of the work as it has come down to us. For one thing the narrative is carried down to 1737 A.V. (1680 A.D.), five years after the poet is said to have completed the work. Lest it be argued that the portions after the consecration may have been added later on, it should be remembered that in several places during the main narrative, the poet mentions Jai Singh as the reigning Rana who, after listening to the work, ordered it to be inscribed on stone[22]. It is true that in most cases these verses occur at the end of cantos and may therefore be claimed as later additions to the original version of these cantos. But cantos XVII to XXI describe what happened on the day of the consecration and thereafter

15. V, 43. 45, 46.

16. VI, 27, 28.

17. VI, 37, 38, 39.

18. VI, 45, 46.

19. Raj Singh's reign is famous for the large number of literary works.

20. Ranchhod 1, 10.

21. Ibid V, 52.

22. Ibid V, 52; VIII, 53, XVIII, 39; X, 43. says that the Rana who asked me to compose the Praśasti, heard it and gave orders that it be inscribed on stone.

in connecion with the dedication ceremony. These could not have been composed by or on the day of the consecration.

The original version ready on the day of the dedication for example, could not have included Ranchhod Bhatt's mission bearing gifts to Raja Jaswant Singh of Jodhpur. It will have to be admitted that the date of the commencement of the work and the date of its completion given in the work are examples of poetic licence and cannot be taken to be true.

It is possible to presume that the work was composed in parts. The first five pre-Raj Singh cantos could have been written any time. Cantos VI to VIII deal with Raj Singh's reign prior to his decision to construct the dam. They again can be put anywhere. But events described in cantos IX and X, took place in or after 1718 A. V. (1661 A. D.) and could only have been put together after they had taken place. Canto XI gives the measurements of the construction when complete, canto XII among other things names the villages which were submerged in the lake obviously when the construction was complete. Cantos XIII to XVII describe what happened before or on the day of the consecration.

But one fact about the date of the composition stares up in the face and cannot be easily forgotten. If the work was commissioned by Raj Singh when he began the construction of the dam and was ready on the day of the consecration in whatever stage, how is it that no gift to the author, howsoever small, finds a mention in the narrative? Ranchhod's mission to Jodhpur is mentioned but there is nothing about his receiving any recognition from Raj Singh for the work. It seems a safe guess that probably Ranchhod completed the work in the reign of Jai Singh who, as our author asserts, after hearing it, ordered it to be inscribed on stone and placed the inscriptions where they are to be found today. The narrative closes with the treaty of peace between Aurangzeb and the Rajputs in 1680 when Jai Singh had been on the throne for a very short period. The hero of the Mahākāvya is Raj Singh. His son would consider it an act of piety, paying his debt to the memory of his father to publish this account of the great enterprise where it would live for ages. Verse 43 of Canto X seems to bear out this suggestion where it is said that the

Rana who ordered the work to be composed, heard it and had it inscribed on stone. Jai Singh is not mentioned here by name but as the author asserts earlier,[23] it was undoubtedly Jai Singh who had the work inscribed on stone, but he could not have been the Rana who ordered it to be composed as well. The work as it stands goes beyond the death of Raj Singh. He could not have ordered it to be incised on stone, though he could have easily ordered the composition.

Not to loose the merit of teaching it to a pupil, as Vālmīki is said to have taught Lava and Kusha, sons of Rama to sing his *Rāmāyaṇa*, the author complicates the issues still further by asserting here and there that he composed the present work for (or while teaching) his brother Lakshman and Bharat and for the benefit of students like his sons[24]. As the verse declaring that Raj Singh ordered him to compose the present work comes immediately after, it is difficult to be sure what the author wants us to believe.

The work itself can be divided into three main parts. The introduction brings the story upto the end of the reign of Raj Singh's father Jagat Singh covering the first five contos. The second portion, from cantos VI to XVI tell the story of the earlier years of Raj Singh's reign and of the planning, building and the dedication of the dam that created the Rajasmund. Cantos XVII to XXIII. bring the history of Mewar after the dedication of the dam to the conclusion of the peace between Aurangzeb and the Rajputs, and together with the concluding canto XXIV form the third portion of the work. This leaves out the first slab which the poet has himself kept out of his numbered cantos. It is mostly in the form of a *mangalā caraṇa,* invoking the blessings of a host of gods and goddesses for the enterprise. Probably at some stage in the composition of the work the author thought the verses included in the first canto for the purpose were not enough for such a large work and decided to add one full canto for the job.

The inscription seems to have first come to the notice

23. Ibid, V, 52, VIII, 53. The Epigraphia Indica edition reads it only as Si but the text as reproduced in the Vir Vinod reads clearly jay
24. Ibid, I, 9; XXIV, 16.

of two Britishers, Major Bruce and Captain Blair of the Political Department stationed in Rajputana. They arranged for a transcription of the work which Captain Blair undertook to translate into English. Their labour seems to have been wasted on account of their death before this enterprise could be carried out. Munshi Devi Prashad of Jodhpur, to whom Indian history owes so much, however published an Urdu and Hindi abridgement of the work in 1884 in the series of monthly booklets which he had started publishing by then. Though a great Persian scholar and very well read in the history of medieval India, he was not a student of Sanskrit. His publication of the abridgement in Urdu and Hindi script was defective in many respects. Its publication by the Naval Kishore Press of Lucknow did not rouse much interest in scholarly circles. The press was well known for its publications of Persian texts and their translations. It had published Urdu translations of some of the religious books of the Hindus but no Sanskrit scholar felt drawn to its publications. The Persian-knowing students of history looked upon the work as an oddity in Sanskrit literature, a long text on stone.

Swami Dayanand Sarasvati during his peregrinations in Rajputana had tried to rouse the interest of the Rajput rulers in their ancient history. His exhortations brought fruit in the setting up of historical departments in Udaipur and Jodhpur. In Udaipur, one of his disciples, Kaviraj Shyamal Das whom he named as one of his trustees in his will, had risen to be the Dewan. Maharana Fateh Singh of Udaipur, who also respected Swami Dayanand as his Guru, entrusted the work of writing a comprehensive history of Rajputana to Kaviraj Shyamal Das. He built in the Raj Vilas Library, Udaipur, a very good collection of Sanskrit and Persian works which he used in his *Vīr Vinod*,[25] History of Rajputana, running into seven quarto volumes. The work is all the more valuable in that it reproduced in original or translations quite a lot of original material. So included in the work was the text of the *Rājapraśasti Mahākāvyam* reproduced in a volume published in 1887.

25. This work has been described in my *Maharana Pratap* and *Bibliography of Mughal India*.

The work was printed by the Udaipur State in the eighties. Soon after, it acquired a political, nay a money, value which the State had not foreseen. In claims about jagirs the claimants started citing it as their authority for the claims they preferred. If they could prove from the narration in the *Vīr Vinod* that an ancestor of theirs was present in a particular battle, they could press their claim for a grant which they claimed had been made to their family for fighting heroically in that battle. The Maharana thereupon stopped the publication of the work and its printed copies went into a storehouse in the State. A copy was kept in the confidential despatch box of the Maharana who is said to have consulted it himself when disposing of cases regarding claims for jagirs. Thus the complete printed text of the *Rājapraśasti* remained unavailable to scholars.

Pandit Gauri Shanker Ojha who had worked in Udaipur for some time brought the present work to the notice of scholars in his *Bulletin of the Rajputana Museum* in 1918. Later on, he used it extensively in his *History of Rajputana.*

I acquired a handwritten transcript of the *Vīr Vinod* for the Lal Chand Library, D.A.V. College, Lahore. A proof copy of the work had found its way to the library of the Nagri Pracharani Sabha, Banaras. My transcript was copied from the Banaras printed text. It was then that the inscription came to my notice and I decided to get it published. That great orientalist, Dr. A. C. Woolner, was then the Vice-Chancellor of the Panjab University, Lahore and he readily agreed to help me in this work. The government of Maharana Sir Bhupal Singh of Udaipur got interested in the work and he graciously extended all help to me in the matter. The Curator of the State Museum and a Shastri in the Service of the State were deputed to assist me in my study of the inscription. In the summer of 1935, we studied the inscription together at Raj Nagar, prepared some ink estampages of the inscription and compared the inscribed text with the copy of the text as printed in the *Vīr Vinod.*

On my return to Lahore Dr. Woolner accepted the work for publication in the Panjab University Oriental Series. On this the Sanskrit text was sent to the press.

On account of my other preoccupations, the printing

of the Sanskrit text took a long time, but the entire stock of the complete printed text was destroyed at Lahore during the partition riots in 1947. Once again the printed text disappeared.

The Archaeological Department of the Government of India had also got interested in the work and had taken inked estampages of the inscription in 1934. It started publishing the work in *Epigraphia Indica* as an inscription. The publication was spread over several numbers and was completed in Vols XXX and XXXI of the *Epigraphia Indica.*

In the pages that follow I have made use of the text printed in the *Epigraphia Indica,* a file copy of the text in my possession of the edition in the Panjab University Oriental Publications Fund Series, and the text as reproduced in the *Vir Vinod.*

CHAPTER II

TRADITIONAL HISTORY OF THE RULING DYNASTY

As is usual in this type of composition, the long genealogy of the reigning ruler Jai Singh given in *Rājapraśasti* is partly mythical, partly legendary and only partly historical. The *Vāyū Purāṇa*, the *Bhāgavata Purāṇa* and the *Mahābhārata*[26] are relied upon for regaling the reader with an account of 92 generations of rulers of Ayodhya, from Manu to Brihadbala, who is said to have been killed in the great battle by Arjuna's son, Abhimanyu. Another 30 rulers see the end of the Ikṣvāku line at Ayodhya with Sumitra as the last ruler.

The next ruler, Vijaya, left Ayodhya for the south and obeying a heavenly command added *āditya* to the names of the new line. Where he settled we are not told. [27] Fourteen generations of Ādityas followed in the south. Then the suffix Āditya was dropped by the descendants of the last of these, Grahāditya. He seems to have founded a new dynasty of Grahaputras[28] (Guhilautas in the local version.)

His eldest son Vāshpa, wise beyond his years, practised such austerities at Nagahradapur (probably Nagada) that a gratified Śiva bestowed the lordship of Chitrakuta (Chitor) on him and his descendants while Vāshpa was only fifteen. The boon was granted to him on 7 Sudi Magh. 91 (?). He had to fight hard to turn the boon into a reality. But he soon succeeded in defeating and driving out Manuraja of Chitrakut and established himself there taking the title Raval.[29]

26. Ranchhod, I, 19, 11, 31, II, 24, 25.

27. Canto II gives the genealogy upto Vijaya.
Vijaya's going to the south is mentioned in verse 36 of canto II and his addition of Āditya to his name in verse 37.

28. Ibid. Verse 6 of Canto II. starts the Grahaputra line.

29. Ibid, III, 6 to 19. Vāshp is Bapa of Rajput tradition. Though oral and local tradition puts his assuming royal authority in the year 191, it does not seem that the year indicated is the Vikram era. But as we know of no other era current in this part of the country, Ojha assured that the date was in the Vikram era and to get over the difficulty that a later and more authentic tradition places Bapa in the eighth century, he proposed that the year should be read as 791 A.V. instead of 191. (Udaipur, I, 110.).

Now followed a line of rulers some of whom are otherwise known to history. Vāshpa was followed by his son Khumāna whom Govinda succeeded. Mahendra, Alu, Singhavarman Sālivahāna, Naravahana, Ambāpraśāda, Kirtivarman, Naravarman, Narapati, Uttama, Bhairava, Panjarāja, Karnāditya, Bhava Singh, Gotrasingha, Hansarāja, Subhagarāja, Vairda, Varisingh, Tej Singh and Samar Singh[30] followed one after another. Samar Singh married Prithi, sister of Prithvi Raj of Delhi who fought against Shihab-ud-Din Ghori whom on the authority of the *Raso* (*Prithviraj Raso*) Samar Singh is said to have captured. This seems to have availed him nothing. He was himself killed in action, whether in the same battle[31] or in the one that followed the author does not make clear.

Under Samar Singh's son Karn there again came a parting of ways. One of his sons, Māhapa, established himself at Dungarapur[32]. The second, Rāhapa, defeated Mohkam Singh of Mandsor and was allowed to assume the higher title of Rana which the vanquished Mohkam Singh and his predecessors had enjoyed. Having spent sometime at Sisoda, his decendants at Chitor came to he called Sisodias[33].

Narapati, Jasakarna, Nāgapāl, Punyapāl, Prithvimal, Bhuvani Singh, Bhim Singh, Jaya Singh, Lakshman Singh followed one after another. The last was a contemporary of Ala-ud-Din. His younger brother was Ratansi whose beloved Padmini was. On her account Ala-ud-Din beseiged Chitrakuta. In the battle that followed Lakshman Singh perished along with his twelve brothers and seven sons[33].

30. Ranchhod, III, 20 to 23.

31. Ibid, III, 24 to 27. Ranchhod here wrongly follows *Prithviraj Raso*. Epigraphical evidence however goes against him. Now that the historicity of the *Raso* and its composition by a court poet of Prithvi Raj has been successfully challenged, we can excuse the author for following a work which must have been well known in his times and respected very much. Samar Singh was not even a contemporary of Prithvi Raj. He was alive in 1285 A.D. when he is mentioned as the reigning ruler in the Abu inscription of 1342.

32. Ibid, III, 28 to 34.

33. Ibid, IV, 1 to 7.

Here again we are in deep waters. Probably because Samar Singh has been made a contemporary of Prithvi Raj, eleven generations are said to separate him from Ratansi, Ala-ud-Din's contemporary. But if, as epigraphical evidence points out, Samar Singh was alive in 1258 eleven

He was followed by his nephew Hamira, son of his eldest brother Arasi.

The crystal figure of Lakshmi (in the temple of Ekalingaji) had been deposited in the indrasarasa lake (during he Muslim occupation of Chitor). When all efforts to recover the image failed, Hamira had an image of Śiva with our faces and an image of Parvati, both in black stone, installed in the temple of Ekalingaji.

He was followed on the throne of Chitor by Kshetra Singh, Lakha and Mokala one after another. Mokala had a tank constructed at Nagarbada (Nagda) and named it after his younger brother Bagh, Baghela. He added a marble enclosure to Ekalinga temple[34]. He went on a long pilgrimage to Dwaraka and Samkhadhar[35] (in the gulf of Cutch).

He was followed by his son, Kumbhakarn who built the fort Kumbhalgarh[36]. His son Rayamall succeeded him.

Rayamall's son Sangram Singh expanded his dominion to Fatehpur in the territories Babar had inherited from Ibrahim Lodhi. His dominion extended right up Prilyakhala[37] (the Pili river near Bayana).

His sons Ratan Singh, Vikramaditya and Udai Singh followed him one after another. Udai Singh had an artificial

generations cannot be squared in between 1258 and 1313 when Ala-ud-Din attacked Chitor. Ranchhod himself elsewhere mentions only 3 rulers, Ajesi, (Ajai Singh), Kheta and Kakha, between Samarsi and Hamir (canto XX, verses 48 to 50). All authorities and Rajput traditions agree that Hamnir turned out the Delhi administrators whom Ala-ud-Din had stationed ih Mewar. So going backwards to Samarsi we have Lakhshman Singh, Kheta and Ajasi. Kheta we know from other sources was Hamir's son. So only two generations separate Samarsi and Hamir. Ajesi (Ajai Singh) and Lakshman Singh Ala-ud-Din's adversary at Chitor. It is interesting to note that Ranchhod makes Lakshman Singh Ala-ud-Din's adversary at Chitor and makes Padmani, his younger brother Ratan Singh's wife. Epigraphical evidence makes Ratan Singh, Samar Singh's son and mentions Lakshman Singh as a defender of Chitor after Ratan Singh's death (*Kumbhal Garh Inscription, verses* 176 *to* 180). Earlier Rajput scurces do not make any mention of Padmani in connection with Ala-ud-Din's attack. But Ranchhod's contemporary, Nensi, brings her in. He however mentions Ratansi as the ruler and Lakshman Singh as his brother. Surprisingly this fact finds no mention in Ojha's History of Udaipur. The account of Padmani that Tod handed down from tradition based on a hazy knowledge of the story of *Padmavat* of Jayasi is entirely wrong.

34. Ibid, IV, 7 & 8.

35. Ibid, IV, 10 to 12. Ojha dees not mention his going on pilgrimage nor does he mention the site of the tank.

36. Ibid, IV, 13, 14.

37. Ibid, IV, 14 to 16.

the same[46]. Jagat Singh died on 10 April, 1652 and Raj Singh succeeded him.

Raj Singh's Accession

Born on 4 October, 1629, he was barely twenty three when his father died. As usual the coronation ceremony was deferred to an auspicious day fixed by the court astrologers who chose 25th February, 1653 as the auspicious day when Raj Singh was crowned with due ceremonials. He was weighed against silver which was given away in charity.

It was customary for a new Maharana to set out for the temple of Eklingji soon after coronation. In law god Ekling was the ruler of Mewar. When a newly crowned Maharana came to the temple, he performed the usual acts of worship at the temple whereupon the Mahant of the temple, would proclaim him the new Diwan—prime minister—of Mewar on behalf of the god. To mark the occassion, the Maharana was presented a robe of honour, a sword, a royal umbrella, a chamar to keep away flies, as the signs of office. Like his predecessors Raj Singh went to pay due homage to the god and was inducted into the office of the Diwan with due ceremonies.

An inscription (now in the Victoria Museum, Udaipur) was discovered in a debris on a platform facing the temple of the Naths in the vicinity of the temple of Eklingji several years ago. This proclaimed that on a pilgrimage to Ekling Temple, Raj Singh had himself weighed against jewels or precious stones. The inscription does not give the date of the visit. Ojha puts it as soon after Raj Singh's accession. As we have seen above Raj Singh had himself weighed against silver at the time of his coronation. It is not likely that he would mark a later visit to the Eklingji with a very much larger amount given in charity than what he spent at the time of his formal coronation. Neither *Raj Vilas* nor Ranchhod mentions his making such a huge gift. Had Raj Singh done so, Ranchhod could not have omitted the fact. The authenticity of the inscription itself is in doubt, but even if it were genuine, that would not necessarily prove that such a gift was made. It is as easy to exaggerate things when a

Pratap thereafter lived in peace at Udaipur, while eightyfour of his chiefs settled at Kosithal. Pratap Singh once presented his turban to a bard who happened to please him. When the bard appeared at the court of the Mughal emperor at Delhi, while saluting, he took off his turban and then bowed down to the emperor in salute. When the emperor asked him why he had behaved in that manner, the bard explained that the turban he was wearing had once adorned Rana Pratap's head, so while bowing down he had kept it aloft in his hand. Pratap became known as unbendable[42].

Amar Singh followed Pratap. In his fight against the Mughals, Amar Singh faced Khurram, Jahangir's son, and Abdulla Khan and Qaim Khan. He killed the last named officer in an engagement at Untala and took back Malpura. His son, Karn Singh, plundered Sironj, Malva, and Dhamdhemra and gathered rich spoils. Jahangir made peace with Amar Singh. Khurram and Amar Singh met at Goghunda where a treaty was signed. Thereafter Amar Singh lived in peace at Udaipur[43].

42. Ibid, IV 36 to 50.

It is difficult to identify Serima of Ranchhod. No uncle of Akbar (or of Jahangir) of that name (or of any variation of that name) can be traced in contemporary records. It is surprising that Ranchhod who wrote two histories of Mewar should have made no attempt at gathering authentic news of what had happened only a century ago. Expeditions led by lesser leaders often get described as led by the Mughal emperor in local histories. But Ranchhod's embroiling of Salim and Serima, a son and an uncle of the reigning emperor, in this way is probably a unique achievement.

43. Ibid, V, 1 to 9.

The treaty between Amar Singh and Jahangir was supposed to govern Mughal-Mewar relations. When Shahjahan invaded Mewar in 1654 he alleged the infringement of the treaty by Raj Singh as his reasons for the attack. Aurangzeb promised Raj Singh all the honours Amar Singh had enjoyed if Raj Singh would side with Aurangzeb in his rebellion against Shahjahan. Jahangir's *Memoirs*, I, 134 mentions two main obligations the Rana undertook. The fort of Chitor was not to be repaired and the Rana was to keep a contingent of 1000 horse in the imperial service. The Farman has been reproduced in the *Vīr Vinod*, I.

Karn Singh, his son, followed him. He helped Akheraja of Sirohi, defeating his rivals[44]. When Khurram rebelled against his father, Karn Singh gave him refuge in his own palace. When Jahangir died, Karn made his brother, Arjun, accompany Khurram in his march to Delhi. Arjun was present at the coronation ceremony of Shahjahan[45].

44. Ibid, V, 10 to 12.
45. Ibid, V, 18, 14.

CHAPTER III

MAHARANA RAJ SINGH

Maharana Jagat Singh

Karn Singh was followed by his son Jagat Singh who had been born in 1664 A. V. (1607 A. D.). He ascended the throne on 3 Śudi Baisakh 1685 (May 8, 1628). He was a great warrior. He sent his minister, Akheraja against Rao Punja of Dungarpur. Unable to stand against the Mewar army, Rao Punja fled. Akheraja plundered Dungarpur and returned to Udaipur. Rathor Ram Singh attacked Deolia, killed its chief Ravat Jasvant Singh and his son in battle. Deolia yielded rich booty in plunder. Jogat Singh attacked Sirohi next and vanquished Rao Akheraj and annexed a part of Sirohi territory which Akheraj had seized from Toga Balisa. Jagat Singh's Divan was next sent against Bhag Chand, chief of Banswara. Bhag Chand was defeated and made to acknowledge Jagat Singh's sovereignty and pay him Rs two lacs.

Jagat Singh was very generous in his gifts. After his accession he gave away silver worth his weight every year till June, 1647. On the solar eclipse occurring in that year on 22 June, 1647, he had himself weighed against gold and gave it all away in charity. Thenceforward he had himself similarly weighed against gold every year. He added a gold cupola to the temple of Jagan Nath on the occasion of the marriage of his daughter to Bhavani Singh, son of Rao Chhatar Sal of Bundi in 1704 A. V. Jagat Singh's mother Jambuvati was very fond of going on pilgrimage. She celebrated Diwali of 1698 A. V. at Dwaraka and made large gifts. In 1704 A. V. she went on a more extensive pilgrimage visiting Mathura and Gokula at the time of Diwali and visited Śukra Prayaga, Kashi, Ayodhya and several other centres of pilgrimage. Wherever she went not only did she make large gifts but persuaded her companions to do

46. Ibid, V, 13, 19, 20, 21, 25, 27, 28, 34, 30, 31, 32, 38 to 44.

the same[46]. Jagat Singh died on 10 April, 1652 and Raj Singh succeeded him.

Raj Singh's Accession

Born on 4 October, 1629, he was barely twenty three when his father died. As usual the coronation ceremony was deferred to an auspicious day fixed by the court astrologers who chose 25th February, 1653 as the auspicious day when Raj Singh was crowned with due ceremonials. He was weighed against silver which was given away in charity.

It was customary for a new Maharana to set out for the temple of Eklingji soon after coronation. In law god Ekling was the ruler of Mewar. When a newly crowned Maharana came to the temple, he performed the usual acts of worship at the temple whereupon the Mahant of the temple, would proclaim him the new Diwan—prime minister—of Mewar on behalf of the god. To mark the occassion, the Maharana was presented a robe of honour, a sword, a royal umbrella, a chamar to keep away flies, as the signs of office. Like his predecessors Raj Singh went to pay due homage to the god and was inducted into the office of the Diwan with due ceremonies.

An inscription (now in the Victoria Museum, Udaipur) was discovered in a debris on a platform facing the temple of the Naths in the vicinity of the temple of Eklingji several years ago. This proclaimed that on a pilgrimage to Ekling Temple, Raj Singh had himself weighed against jewels or precious stones. The inscription does not give the date of the visit. Ojha puts it as soon after Raj Singh's accession. As we have seen above Raj Singh had himself weighed against silver at the time of his coronation. It is not likely that he would mark a later visit to the Eklingji with a very much larger amount given in charity than what he spent at the time of his formal coronation. Neither *Raj Vilas* nor Ranchhod mentions his making such a huge gift. Had Raj Singh done so, Ranchhod could not have omitted the fact. The authenticity of the inscription itself is in doubt, but even if it were genuine, that would not necessarily prove that such a gift was made. It is as easy to exaggerate things when a narration is inscribed on stone as when it is committed to paper.

The Rana of Udaipur was also a Mughal mansabdar. As such the accession of every new Maharana had to be regularised by the Mughal emperor by conferring a rank on the new Rana. Unlike custom in other states, Mewar had maintained the succession to the state in its own hands. The son—the eldest son—immediately succeeded his father. He was formally crowned in the state. The visit to Eklingji conferred the office of the Diwan to the god on him. The Mughal recognition came last of all. It was on 19 April, 1653 that Shahjahan formally recognised Raj Singh's accession by issuing a royal order conferring on him the rank of a 5000 soldier, and a commando of 5000 horse and gave him Mewar as his hereditary *jagir*. There was an interval of more than a year between Jagat Singh's demise and Raj Singh's recognition by the emperor. But this 'lacuna' did not create any difficulty. The Maharana's home territories had never been given to any one else. It was not likely that any Hindu mansabdar would accept a jagir in Mewar.

Mewar Sardars

When Raj Singh ascended the throne, Mewar had been in alliance with the Mughal emperors for less than half a century. But Mewar tradition kept the Maharana in Mewar and the ruler never left the state nor did he accept any command outside the state. In accordance with the treaty between Rana Amar Singh and Jahangir, the Rana did keep a Mewar contingent for service in the Mughal army. Its usual strength was 1000 horse and a prince of the ruling house usually served as its leader. As opportunities for advance in Mughal service for intrepid warriors were many, sometimes a Mewar sardar would leave the state to seek a career for himself outside in the Mughal service. The Mewar contingent is known to have been present in many Mughal expeditions in and outside India. When Khurram rebelled against his father, Jahangir, one of his trustiest and most valiant lieutenant was Raja Bhim of Mewar. Khurram had sought refuge at Udaipur during his rebellion for some time. Naturally Shahjahan could ill afford to pick up a quarrel either with his host of his days of rebellion Rana Karn Singh, or with his son, Jagat Singh.[47] This however, did not prevent him from taking into his service such discontended Mewar chiefs as sought such service at his court.

Mewar was a Rajput state little affected by Mughal traditions and customs. The Rana was the head of the ruling clan and at the head of other Rajput clans in his own state. But the members of the clans and other Rajputs had their well defined status in the state. A tradition seems to maintian that 'sardars'—chiefs, heads of families—in Mewar stood divided in 3 classes. Appropriating a Mughal designation, those of the highest class came to be designated as 'Umra' vulgarised as 'Umrao'.

Rather strangely the first place among the Mewar sardars was occupied by Rajputs who did not belong to the ruling clan, jhalas of *Bari Sadarī*. Their ancestor had been driven out of his principality in Gujarat. When he sought refuge at Mewer, Rana Raimal had appointed Ajja, his prime minister. His descendants served the rulers of Mewar so well that one of them, Raj Singh married a daughter of Rana Karn Singh. Jhala Chandar and Jhala Var Singh are mentioned as ehiefs of Sadari in the *Rājapraśasti*.

The second in rank were the Chauhans of Bedala. The family had settled in Mewar after the battle of Khanwah between Baber and Rana Sanga. As was the case with the Jhalas, the ancestor of these Chauhans had been a ruling prince and this accounts for the place the family came to occupy in the Udaipur heirarchy. These Chauhans had first settled at Begun, but Rana Karn Singh, Raj Singh's grandfather, had given Bedala to Rao Baloo when he pursuaded him to return to Mewar from Delhi. Rao Ram Chandar was the chief of the clan when Raj Singh ascended the throne

47. Ranchhod does not mention the date of Jagat Singh's death. *Vir Vinod* puts it on 10 April, 1652. Shahjahan received the news of his death on 27 October, 1652, (Waris, 68b). The date of the coronation ceremony is mentioned by Ranchhod, VI, 11. It seems that, as usual, Raj Singh reported his accession to power after his coronation to the emperor and sent a present. The report and the present were formally received in the court on 28 March, 1653. (Waris 73b). It took the emperor more than three weeks to issue the royal order conferring the rank of 5000 er on Raj Singh. Waris (73 b) reports this being done on 19 April 1653.

and was succeeded by Saval Singh. Rao Kesari Singh is also mentioned in the inscription.

Third in rank came Chauhans of Kotharaya under Rukman God. He and his son played an important part in the difficult days of Mewar-Mughal struggle.

Chandavats of Solambra came next. Though fourth in rank, they enjoyed the proud privilege of fighting in the van of Mewar's battles. Ravat Raghunath Singh was their chief when Raj Singh became the Maharana. He and his son Ratan Singh fought valiantly for Mewar. Kesari Singh has also been mentioned in the inscription.

The Panwar chief of Bajolia, Vairisal, was a maternal uncle of Maharana Raj Singh and traced his ancestory to Ashok who had left Jagnor to fight under Rana Sanga at Khanwaha.

Sangavats of Devalgarh represented another branch of the ruling family. They were descendants not of Rana Sanga but of Sanga of Deogarh who was a great grandson of Rao Chunda. Gokal Das and Dwarka Das were the chiefs of Deogarh during the reign of Raj Singh and Jai Singh.

Ravat Hari Singh, the chief of Begun represented another offshoot of the reigning house. The family rose to eminence in Maharana Amar Singh's reign when Megh Singh expelled the Mughal jagirdar- another member of the reigning family—from Begun and brought it under Mewar once again. Megh Singh had himself been buffeted enough by fate, but this did not prevent him from sowing seeds of discord by nominating his younger son, Raj Singh, as his successor, keeping out his eldest son. Narsingh Das. It fell upon Maharana Raj Singh to bring about a peaceful settlement of the question by giving a Jagir to the eldest son at Gothlai so that he would leave his younger brother in peace at Begun.

The Rajrana of Delwara was another offshoot of the Jhalas of Sadari. Kalyan Singh was the head of these descendants of Sajja now. His son Ragho Dev and his grandson Jai Singh played their part in contemporary Mewar warfare.

The Ravat of Amet was also a member of the ruling clan. His anccstor Patta had been left by Rana Udai Slngh to defend Chitor along with Jaimal Rathor against Akbar. Madho Singh was the head of the family at this time.

The jagir of Gogunda had been created but recently by Maharana Amar Singh's bestowing the place on Jhala Kanha Singh. His successor Jaswant Singh was the Jagirdar of Gogunda at this time.

Kanor was held by Ajjavats. The family chief held the title of Ravat. Man Singh was at this time head of the branch.

Bhindor was held by the Shaktavat branch of the reinging house. 'Maharaj' Saval Singh and 'Maharaj, Mahkam Singh were the heads of the family one after another under Raj Singh.

Badnor had been conferred on Manwar Das, a Mertia Rathor, by Maharana Pratap. His son Thakur Sanval Das was the head of the family when Raj Singh ascended the throne.

Ravats of Bansi represented another cadet house of the ruling dynasty—descendants of Shakt Singh, son of Maharana Udai Singh. Ravat Jaswant Singh and his son, Kesari Singh, were the head of Bansi house one after another.

Raos of Parsoli werc Chauhans. This 'Thikana' was a creation of Raj Singh himself as also those of Lasami, Dabla, Bhadu. Naval Singh was the Thakur of Sardargarh during Raj Singh's reign.

Hathi Singh was probably the Ravat of Pipalya when Raj Singh became the ruler. This house also was an offshoot of the royal family.

Vir Bhan Rathor was the Thakur of Kelva at this time and Chandar Singh chief of Bambori.

The descendants of ViramDev, a son of Maharana Udai Singh, enjoyed the right to command the garrison at Kumbhal Garh.

Vika of Rup Nagar was the Solanki Thakur of Rup Nagar, Mahesh Das, the Maharaj of Mangroh, and Bhim Singh Rathor held Nimari. [47a]

Mewar of Raj Singh was an extensive state. But Mandal Garh, Banera, Shahpura. Dungarpur and Banswara,

47a. This account is based on *Vir Viond.*

seem to have assumed a status of independence as far as Mewar was concerned, they were held by chiefs who held jagirs under the Mughal Emperors. Mewar had not given up its claims against them and we shall find Raj Singh waging war against some of them, in these territories and succeeding in at least exacting tribute, when not incorporating them, in his own state.

Since Rana Udai Singh's time Udaipur had been the capital of the state, though past tradition still clung to Chitor to give it a pride of place. Akbar had taken the fort, during the seige it had suffered much damage. Age in its own turn had made some of its defences useless whereas past experience convinced Maharana Jagat Singh that on some sides it required being strengthened. Though the treaty with the Mughals had laid down that Chitor's defences were not to be put in order, Jagat Singh had taken the plunge, repaired the portions which needed looking after and added to the defences by raising the walls on the side on which they were too low to serve their purpose. Obviously Jagat Singh was entertaining no rebellious designs, he had simply done what it seemed needed to be done to allow Chitor to continue to occupy the place tradition demanded it should.

The Last Sack of Chitor

Raj Singh had not been on the throne of Mewar for two years when he heard of Shahjahan's leaving Delhi for Ajmer on 7th November 1654[48] and of his giving orders to Saadullah Khan to move to Chitor which he was instructed to attack and destroy[49].

On Maharana's request Chandar Bhan was sent as a mediator to Udaipur[50]. He told the Rana that he had offended the emperor by several acts of his[51]. He had added to, repaired and strengthened the fort at Chitor[52]. Its

48. Ranchhod, VI, 11, 12.

49. Shah Jahan's intention to move against Udaipur had become known earlier when Jai Singh of Jaipur received a royal order dated 13 September, 1654 telling him that he was to join the army that was being sent to Chitor.

50. Cf. Appendix

51. Cf *Jaipur Records*, I, letter received by Jai Singh on 22 October from Dara; Shahjahan to Jai Singh, *Jaipur Records*, II, 221, 222.

52. *Inshai Chandar Bhan* (Ms), folio 3.

western gates that had become useless for want of repairs or otherwise had been repaired and even added to. A new wall 16 yards high had been added on the side of the fort where it had been easy to climb the hill. This wall was sixteen yards wide in some places and 3 to 3½ yards in other places[53]. The fort had been strengthened otherwise on all sides. When Shah Jahan was besieging Qandahar, the Rana had gone into the imperial territories for pilgrimage but with a great retinue of foot soldiers and cavalry. The Rana was further told that Mewar had not been regularly maintaining an agent of his at the imperial court. The contingent which the Rana had sent for the seige of Qandahar had been insufficient. Waris tells us that in 1652 the Mewar contingent at Qandahar was commanded by Sohal Singh Sasodia who was a commander of 2500 horse. In 1653 a contingent of 1000 horse was present there under Bhupat[54]. Raj Singh told Chandar Bhan that most of these things had been done by his father but he was prepared to stand the blame himself[55].

After a good deal of negotiation, tha Rana undertook to send his son to the imperial court[56].

The poet tells us however that the Rana sent Bhatt Madhusudan to Chitor to meet Saadullah Khan. Our author here is probably trying to fasten upon his father a claim which he neither deserved nor had earned. It is preposterous to believe that Mewar was so bankrupt of diplomats as to compell the Rana to send a Bhatt as his chief negotiator to Saadullah Khan. Madhusudan did not even enjoy the status of the Raj Parohita. But even this status would not have given him a claim to speak for the Rana in such difficult times. Saadullah Khan had not simply marched upon Chitor, he had also attacked the fort, taken it and destroyed not only all the additions Jagat Singh had made

53. Waris, 90 b, 91 a. Shahjahan received the report about additions to the fort on 4 September, 1654 before he had left Delhi. Shyamal Das, Ojha and Sharma are all hopelessly confused in their accounts of the event. Ojha makes Shahjahan send Abdul Karim to Chitor while the emperor was on his way to Ajmer. *Udaipur*, II, 533.

54. Waris, 6la, 61b, 71a.

55. *Inshai Chandar Bhan*. See appendix.

56. Ranchhod VI, 16.

to the fort but inflicted further serious damage on the earlier structure which had been repaired recently[57]. Further, as contemporary Persian historians tell us, the Rana had sent a mission to Shahjahan[58] towards the end of September, as soon as he had learnt of Shah Jahan's intentions[59]. This mission was received at court in the camp at Khalilpur on 4 October, 1654 and included Ram Chand Chauhan, Ragho Das Jhala, Sanval Das Rathor and Parohit Gharib Das. Orders were then issued to send Chandar Bhan to Rana's Court in order to persuade him to send his eldest son to court and to assign a Mewar contingent for service in the Deccan[60]. Chandar Bhan reached Udaipur on 23 October and was there when Saadullah Khan was at Chitor. Saadullah Khan reached Chitor on 27th October and Shah Jahan reached Ajmer the same day. It is preposterous to believe that the Rana would send a mission to the Mugal commander at Chitor when a negotiator on behalf of the emperor was present at Udaipur. Chandar Bhan succeeded in persuading the Rana on 24 October to accept Shah Jahan's demands. On 2nd November, the Rana is reported to have asked for a suitable officer from the Mughal camp who was to take the Rana's son to court[61].

The dialogue between Saadullah Khan and Madhusudhan that follows seems to be the result of the poet's imagination rather than an account of any negotiations that took place[62]. To assert that 20,000 horsemen of the Rana were

57. Waris (93 a) has it that the fort was entirely razed to the ground but Chandar Bhan says that only additions and strengthened portions were destroyed. Cf appendix.

58. Waris (91 b.): Shahjahan was then on his way to Ajmer. He had ordered the expedition against Chitor earlier on 24 September, 1654 (Waris, 90 b-91 a)

59. *Jaipur Records*, II, 221. 222.

60. Waris, 91 (b)

61. Waris, 92 (a).

62. Ojha saw the difficulty in accepting Ranchhod's statement about Madhusudhan's Mission. Ranchhod (VI, 12. 13) definitely says that the mission was sent to Saadullah Khan after the Rana had heard that Shah Jahan had reached Ajmer and Saadullah Khan Chitor. Ojha's Hindi translation of Ranchhod in note 4, page 535, curiously seems to introduce Chandar Bhan's mission in Ranchhod's text where he does not figure at all. Still more curiously, Ojha translates *Rajapraśasti* (VI, 11, 12) to say that before *Chandar Bhan reached Udaipur* Raj Singh sent Jhala and Madhusudhan to court.

equal to 100,000 horsmen of Shah Jahan would have been extremely foolish when Saadullah Khan had taken Chitor and destroyed all the additions and repairs to the fort. Of course one of the excuses Shah Jahan had given for proceeding so suddenly against Mewar had been the undoubted fact, which our author also mentions, that many persons non-grata at the court of Delhi had sought and found refuge in Mewar[63]. But a representative of the Rana seeking peace could ill afford to pass it as lightly as the poet seems to imply Madhusudan did. It was neither the time nor the place to assert, as our author says Madhusudan did, that God had created these two places, Delhi and Udaipur for Kshatriyas and thereby explain away the complaint. It is much more likely, as Chandar Bhan asserts, that Raj Singh sought safety in stating that he had done nothing of the sort, his father may have done some such thing.

Ranchhod is not clear about how the hostilities terminated. At one place he asserts that Saadullah Khan and Raj Singh met and sorted out the Mughal-Rajput differences[64]. Elsewhere he says that the Rana sent prince Sultan Singh along with several Thakurs to meet Shah Jahan through Dara Shikoh[65]. Saadulla Khan is said to have told Madhusudan that if the Rana's son accompanied him to Shah Jahan's presence the Rana would get back fourteen cities. As we know from other sources[66], the Rana fared very badly in this affair. Though he got back Chitor—hence Ranchod's reference to Shah Jahan's giving 14 cities to the Rana—certain additional territory which had so far been assigned to the rulers of Mewar was now given away to other Rajpur princes. Arjuna, son of Vithal Dass, for example, got Badnor. The Rana saved his honour by insist-

Ojha simply lifted the text of this note from the *Vir Vinod II*, 412 and fitted in the wrong refeɪence to verses 11, 12.

The Vir Vinod does not rest Madhusudan's time of departure on the *Raja Prasasti*. It is Ojha's guess and wrong at that.

63. Ibid VI, 14 to 21.

64. Ibid, VI, 21, 22.

65. Ibid, VI, 24, 25 Chandar Bhan was on the staff of Dara.

66. *Cf. the Last Sack of Chitor* by the present writer, *in the Twentieth Century Allahabad*, July, 1937.

67. *Jaipur Records*, II, 123-125.

ing that his son would leave for Ajmer only after Chitor was actually evacuated by the Mughal commander[68].

Aurangzeb's Rebellion and Mewar

Canto VII and a part of VIII should be reversed in time. When Aurangzeb rebelled against Shah Jahan, he played upon the Rajput memories of Shah Jahan's unprovoked attack earlier on Chitor and his despoiling Mewar of some of the territories outside Mewar proper which the Ranas had earlier governed. Dara had been Shah Jahan's lieutenant at that time. Though Dara had claimed then that he was responsible for averting the great calamity that had undertaken the Rana in the shape of Shah Jahan's attack on Chitor[69], it seems to have been easy to convince the Rana that the attack was inspired by Dara.

Now when Aurangzeb rebelled against Shah Jahan, Aurangzeb reopened correspondence with the Rana. One Indar Bhatt was sent with verbal messages to Raj Singh and instructed to secure verbal assurances from the Rana for helping Aurangzeb[70]. This the Rana seems to have done. But soon another letter followed which assured Raj Singh he would be allowed to resume Pur and Mandal on his fulfilling his engagements. He was instructed to send a contingent under a relation of his[71]. As Raj Singh had still not sent any contingent, we find Aurangzeb still urging the Rana to send immediately a contingent under one of his sons. They were instructed to join Aurangzeb's army after he had crossed the Narbada[72]. But when the battle of Dharmat was fought in May 1658, Aurangzeb's army was still without a Mewar contingent. We find Aurangzeb writing to the Rana and giving him the glad news of his success against Jaswant Singh. Now he formally granted the lost parganas to Raj Singh and asked him to send the Mewar contingent at once[73].

68. Chandar Bhan's letter. Cf. appendix.
Waris, 93 a.

69. *Jaipur Records*, I, 90, 91, Chandar Bhan who negotiated the peace terms was on Dara's staff. Hence the claims.

70. *Vir Vinod*, II, 417. The original letter has been reproduced. here from Udaipur archives.

71. Ibid, II, 419-421.

72. Ibid, II, 421, 422.

73. Ibid, II, 423 to 425.

Raj Singh took full advantage of the opportunity this grant offered him. As Ranchhod says in canto VII, he attacked and overran Dariba, Mandal Garh, Banera, Shahpur, Toda, Mahirab, Malpura, Tonk, Sambhar, Lalsot, and Chatsu[74].

After Aurangzeb entered Agra, Raj Singh sent his brother Arsi and Lal Kanwar to him to offer him felicitations on his ascending the throne. Persian chroniclers do not mention Aurangzeb's bestowing Dungar Pur either on Arsi or Raj Singh though they describe other honours that Aurangzeb bestowed on him and the gifts that he showered on him and .the Rana[75]. Ranchhod's story of Aurangzeb's giving Dungar Pur to Arsi and Arsi's offering it to Raj Singh[76] may read like Bharat and Rama pressing the throne of Ayodhya on each other, but no one could take liberties with Mughal grants in this way.[77] A little later on, Ranchhod asserts that the Rana gave Dungarpur to Raval Girdhar[77]. This naturally implies that Aurangzeb had conferred Dungar Pur on the Rana.

A royal Farman preserved at Udaipur, however, tells us that on 16 August, 1658 Aurangzeb raised Raj Singh to the rank of 6000 er, 6000 horse and gave him additional territory. Badhnor which till then had been held by Raja Jaswant Singh, Mandal which Rup Singh had held, Dungar Pur which Girdhar had held, Banswara which Raval Samarsi had enjoyed, Basawar which Hari Singh Devalaya had governed so far were all conferred upon him. Ghiaspur was also added to him as jagir.[78]

74. Ranchhod, VII, 25 to 42.

75. *Alab-i-Alamgiri*, II, 229 b, 238. Bhim Sen 29, Ranchhod, VIII, 1 to 7. Ranchhod mentions two missions, one under Arsi (1 to 3) another under Sardar Singh (4 to 7). Persian Chroniclers mention Arsi and Rana's son Lal Kanwar together as forming one mission. Lal Kanwar is Sardar Singh of Ranchhod.

76. Ibid, VIII, & 1 to 3.

77. Ibid, VIII, 8

78. The Royal Farman reproduced in *Vir Vinod*, II, 425 to 432, Ojha (*Udaipur*, II, 355, note 2) wrongly argues that to have deserved higher honours. the Rana must have sent a contingent to join Aurangzeb earlier. As stated in the text Aurangzeb was still urging the Maharana to send a contingent after the battle of Dharamat. Persian records do not mention the Maharana sending a contingent before the grant of the

Aurangzeb's war against his brothers gave Raj Singh a very good opportunity of settling old scores. In 1715 A.v. (1658-59 A.D.) he sent an army against Bansvara and made its ruler Samar Singh acknowledge him as his sovereign[79]. His commander, Fateh Singh defeated Hari Singh Devalaya and brought his son Pratap Singh to the Rana's court. Ravat Hari Singh of Mandsor was similarly compelled to accept the Rana as his overlord[80].

Marriage with Rupmati.

The Mughal-Mewar honeymoon did not lost along. In 1717 A. V. (1660 A. D.) Raj Singh proceeded to Kishan Garh and married its ruler, Rup Singh's daughter. Rup Singh had previously promised to give her in marriage to Aurangzeb[82]. Though Ranchhod does not refer to the fact, tradition has it that the princess refused to be wedded to a Muslim and appealed to the Rana to save her from this dishonour. Aurangzeb put her in high dungeon, took away Basawar and Ghiaspur from the Maharana and conferred them on HariSingh who had previously held them.

In 1719 (1662) Raj Singh conquered Mewala from the Minas and placed it under his own chiefs[84].

In 1720 (1663) Raj Singh sent an army under Ram Singh to Sirohi to release Rao Akheraj from capitivity and place him on the throne. He was successful in his mission[85].

honours. The Rana's son who waited upon Aurangzeb was sent by the Rana for felicitating the emperor on his accession. He returned home after receiving due gifts and honours. In his Farman Aurangzeb in August, 1659 is still asking the Rana to send his son to the army (at the head of a contingent). When Dara wrote to Raj Singh for help (letter reproduced in the *Vir Vinod*, II, 432. 433) on 15 January, 1659 he suggested to the Maharana that now that the prince is back home, the Rana could safely send Dara help. If a Mewar contingent had been in Aurangzeb's army, Dara could have hardly asked for help from the Rana. The neutrality of the Rana was in itself a great service in Aurangzeb's relellion to deserve well of him on his succession.

Persian sources tell us however that the Maharan's cousin, Manahar Das, son of his uncle Gharib Das, went over to Aurangzeb from Murad after Murad's imprisonment by Aurangzeb (*Adāb-i-Ālamgiri*, II 227 (a)

79. Ranchhod, VIII, 8 to 11.
80. Ibid, VIII, 21 to 24.
81. Ibid, VIII, 29 30.
82. Mān, VII, 103 to 128.
83. Maharana's letter preserved in Udaipur Archives reproduced in III, 439 to 442 in original.
84. Ranchhod, VII 30 to 33.
85. Ibid, VIII, 34 to 36 Ojha, History of Sarohi, 254, 108.

Emergence of Nathdwara

When in 1669 Aurangzeb issued a verbal order for the destruction of temples in his dominions, he unwittingly made Mewar the holiest of the holy for the Vaishnvas in central and western India. The famous temple of Viśvanāth at Banaras was demolished by his orders in August 1663. The Gopinath temple suffered the same fate about the same time. Five hundred temples are said to have been destroyed at Banaras though the Jangamvadi temple and the temple of Benimadhava somehow escaped his fury.

Temples at Mathura similarly excited his zeal for the faith and were also destroyed. At Brindaban, priests of the temple of Govardhan, said to have been founded by Vallabhat chārya, fearing such destruction left the temple building to its fate, removed the precious idol and stole out at night. Aurangzeb's orders did not include the temples in the Hindu states. Damodar Lal, the head priest, reached Jodhpur after harrowing adventrues. But Maharaja Jaswant Singh was away on imperial errands. In his absence, his adminstrators were not prepared to give the emperor a cause for complaint by housing the god in exile in their state. In desperation, Damador Lal sent an emissary to Maharana Raj Singh requesting asylum for the exiled god in his state. Raj Singh gladly undertook to do so. From Champasani, where the main party had been left, the priest with his precious burden travelled to the frontiers of Mewar on 5 December, 1671. The Maharana received the party himself when they entered his state. Enough land was settled on the god. The tradition has it that when the party reached Siah, the charoit in which the god was being brought in state stuck deep into mud and try as they might, the attendants were unable to make it move. Happily this was taken to imply that the god did not wish to proceed any further and had chosen the place as his abode. The party settled down there. In due course a temple to house the god was built. The ceremony of installing the god was duly performed on 10 March, 1672. The village was given in gift to the god by the Thakur of Dilwara., Raghudev, who held it then. Its revenue was assessed at Rs. one thousand.

The image of Krishna installed in the temple had been

known as 'Nathji' in its original home at Brindaban. It continued to bear the same name and the village soon came to be known as Nathdwara the portal of Nathji. As such it soon became the holiest shrine of the Vaishnavas in western and central India, converting Mewar into the Mecca of the faithful[85a].

Strangely, this event finds no mention in either our inscription or the contemporary *Raj Vilas*. The gift bestowed on the god was not a royal gift—though it was confirmed by Rana Jagat Singh, the second, in 1793 A.D. (1736-1737 A.D.)[85b]. The emergence of another temple in the state does not seem to have deserved the notice of the contemporaries.

85a. Cf. *Religious Policy of the Mughal Emperor*.
85b. Tod's *Rajasthan*,
Appendix VIII to Chapter XX, page 440. 'Maharana Sh. Jagat Singh II Commanding. The village of Siah in the bills of one thousand rupees yearly rent having been chosen by Nathji for his residence, and given up by Rao Raghudev, I have confirmed it. The Gosain and his heirs shall enjoy it for ever.'

The Nathdwara temple and its Gosain acquired great status in Mewar. Maharana Bhim Singh issued a royal order on Tuesday, Jaisath, shudi 5, 1860 A, V. to all the chieftains, managers of the commands, and of lands granted to the members of the royal household and to all Patels, granting two rupees in every village to Sri Gosainji. Appendix XI to Chapter XX, 441,-Tod's *Rajasthan*,

APPENDIX I

Sweet preparations served on festive occasions

घेवर ! मत्तियूर । षंड ।
यनका । पतासा । गिन्दोरा ।
दह्रिवरा । दोवठा । षाजा
पैरा । खुरम । गुभाषसषस
कलाकन्द । कन्सार । सीरै ।
गुलगुला । सकरपारा । इन्द्रसा ।
पान। ओला । जलेबी हसमी ।
जलेबी अकबरी । जलेबी अमृती ।
पुरी, तिनंगिनी, सेठी, मठी, साबुनी, निषती ।
फेनी । फुनी । रेवरी । घनखडक संठली ।
मुरकी । वरफी। पीलसार। घनसार । संमेती ।
मान, १३३,१३४

APPENDIX II

Chandar Bhan's account of his mission to Udaipur

Architectural Terms used

भूम्यर्द्धम् । पीठम् ।। Verse 3

मेखला । तिलक: ।। Verse 4

संगिकार्यः । स्थरम् ।।। Verse 5

बुरिज । Verse 7

कमल बुरिज । Verse 54

कोष्ठं ।। Verse 7

गर्भंकोष्ठं ।। Verse 9

पूर्वंकोष्ठं ।। Verse 10

मध्यकोष्ठं ।। Verse 50

अन्तःकोष्ठं । Verse 49

सेतुः ।। Verse ।

सोपानमाला । Verse 13

अरहट्टकम् ।। Verse 16

चतुष्की ।। Verse 17

मंडप । सेतुमंडप ।। Verse 51

چہار چمن
(۲۹۳/۶۴ ، آزاد لائبریری)

ذکر فتح قلعه چیتور که از قلعه مشهور هندوستان است وانقیاد و اطاعت زبده راجهای والا تبار رانا راج سنگه بحسن تدبیر ضرب شمشیر عالم گیر

چوں بحر بیکران خاطر دریا مقاطر بادشاه عظیم الشان در ططے بفکری از صایب (40B) موج آں بادشاه آفاق گیر گیتی ستان بمقتضای مصلحتے که مکنون ضمیر آفتاب نظر و مرکوز خاطر ملکوت ناظر بود از دار الخلافه حضرت شاهجهان آباد بلشکر عظیم و سامان و سرانجام که شایان ایں دولت ابد پیوند است فراهم آورده خود بدولت و اقبال و بمبارکی و فیروزی روانه خطه اجمیر گردیدند و دستور اعظم وزیر معظم سعد الله خان را با فواج قاهره منصوره بجانب قلعه چیتور رخصت فرمودند. چوں رانا راج سنگه والد رانا امر سنگه که بر حقیقت تعین افواج نصرت امتزاج اطلاع یافت وکلای معتمد خود را ببارگاه سلاطین پناه فرستاده استعفای تقصیرات خود نموده و از انجا که دریای مکرمت و احسان شاهنشاهی در جوش است عذر جرایم او درجه قبولیت یافت بشرط آنکه جانشین خود را ببارگاه عظمت و جلال بفرستند و عساکر منصوره قلعه چیتور را مسمار نموده برگردند و کمترین ملکان را که در حضرت اهل اعتماد در پیش ایں جماعه واجب الاعتقاد است بعنایت خلعت (41a) مفتخر گردانیده بجهت ابلاغ مژده ایں احسان و آوردن پسر رانا بدرگاه جهان پناه همراه وکلای رانا از حضرت جاه و جلال رخصت فرمودند و بنده عقیدت کیش بسرعت تمام باو دیپور رسیده رانا که پای ثباتش از دهشت افواج قاهره و دهشت عتاب و خطاب بادشاهی متزلزل گشته بود بنصایح ارجمند و سخنان سودمند از اراده تو اتراز کار باز داشت و رانا که گوش سخن شنو و خرد رسا داشت خوانین متفرق خود را جمع و فراهم آورده تکیه بر کرم الهی و عنایت شهنشاهی ساخته جگر گوشه خود را که در سن بیش هشت سالگی بود بعزم

دریافت ملازمت اقدس اعلیٰ روانہ بارگاہ معلّٰی نمود مقارن آں مشیخت مرتبت شیخ عبدالکریم از درگاہ سلاطین پناہ رسید فرمان عالی شان بنام جمدۃ الملکی سعداللہ خان درباب مراجعت لشکر فیروزی اثرآورد وعساکر منصورہ مطابق حکم والا از چیتور معاودت نمود۔ پسر رانا ہمراہ شیخ مذکور وکمترین ملکان بخطہ مرکز اجمیر رسیدہ بملازمت اشرف اعلے مستعد گردیدواز عنایت بخطاب مہانہ (41 ع) وعنایت فیل وخلعت سرفرازی یافت وہمراہنش بمرحمت اسپ وخلعت سربلند گردیدند۔

منشات برہمن

چندر بھان (۲۹۴/۶۴، آزاد لائبریری)

قسم اوّل مشتمل بر نقل عرضداشتی که بدرگاه آسمان جاه ارسال داشته

بجناب بادشاه نویسند:

عرضداشت کمترین بندگان عقیدت نشان چندربھان بعد ازادای لوازم بندگی و عبودیت و تقدیم مراسم اخلاص و عقیدت ذره وار (۵ ۲) بموقف عرض باریافتگان محفل جاه و جلال و استاد های بزم دولت و اقبال میرساند که روز دسهره از خدمت سراسر سعادت مرخص گشته میخواست در عرصه یک هفته بمطلب رسید چون برفاقت کسان زبده راجهای والا اتبار مامور بود بپای آنها طی مسافت نموده روز مبارک دوشنبه بیست و یکم شهر ذی حجه باودیپور رسید آخر روز رانا در جائی که بجهت استقبال مقرر داشت آمده بورود منشور لامع النور و عنایت مرصع مشرف گردید بعد ازادای مراسم اداب کمترین بندگان را بنده درست اعتقاد صافی جناب عالمیان ماب دانسته برخلاف دیگر فرستادهای در کنار گرفت و بتواضعی که در خور فرستادهای آستان دولت نشان باشد پیش آمده در سر سواری حرف زمان تا خانه خود همراه برد. از انجا رخصت نموده روز دیگر در خلوت طلبیده در حضور معتمدان مدارعلیه خود استفسار مضمون احکام لازم الانجام نمود خواست که بر جرایم و تقصیرات خود مطلع گردد بنده بنا بر مزید احتیاط انچه از زبان معجز بیان اشرف اقدس ارفع اعلی ارشاد یافته بود بقید قلم درآورده بود انرا در نظر داشته بزبان قریب الفهم (۱ ۲) عام قریب خاص پسند در گذارش مقدمات لازم الانجام نمود و برانا گفت که الحال وقت شنیدن کلمات هوش افزا است لختی حواس ظاهر و باطن خود را فراهم آورده احکام جهان مطالعه را بگوش هوش شنوید و بر تقصیرات پدر خود و خود مطلع شوید۔ اوّل تقصیری که از پدر شما و شما بوقوع آمده ساختن قلعه چیتور است در واقعه که قلعه را بادشاهان آفاق ستان بضرب شمشیر عالمگیر مفتوح ساخته و خراب مطلق گردانیده بخاک برابر ساخته باشند و روز اول این شرط بمیان آمده باشد که اصلا جائی دران قلعه نسازند و تعمیر نکنند و مرمت ننماید بلکه پرامون ان نگردند چنانچه بهست بحال دارند و هیچ تصرف دران نکنند پاس این حکم نداشته ان عهد موکد را فراموش گردانیده و چشم بصیرت

پوشیده از قبح این افعال نه اندیشیده شروع در ساختن جاها نموده و بمرور ایام کار باینجا رسانیده باشند داخل چه حساب و شایسته کدام عقل دوربین است و این تقصیر عظیم است که از پدر شما و شما که هم در زندگی پدر شریک این مصلحت بودند و بعد از پدر دست درین کار داشته اید بظهور آمده در درگاه سلاطین پناه هیچ تقصیری عظیم تر ازین نیست و (۳۵) که اندیشه خلاف عهد و حکم و قول بخاطر کسی بگذرد دیگر آنکه در حینی که رایات جاه و جلال از مستقر دار الخلافت بعزم مهمی بسرحد دورد ست تشریف برده باشند از او دیپور با جمعیت بسیار سوار و پیاده برآمدن در آمدن بملک بادشاهی و آن را زیارت (و)[۱] غسل گنگ نامیدن حمل بر چه توان نمود و پیش بادشاهان عظیم الشان در معاملات ملکی این تقصیر است دیگر آنکه بر عالم و عالمیان ظاهر است که این دولت خداداد مرجع ما. بادشاهان هفت اقلیم است و امروز سلطانان و خانان و مرزایان عراق و خراسان و ماوراء النهر و بلخ و بدخشان و کاشغر وغیر آن در رکاب ظفر انتساب کمر خدمت بسته حاضر اند بنا راان[۲] دکهن که حلقه بندگی در گوش و غاشیه انقیاد بر دوش این درگاه سلاطین پناه دارند چه رسد و در هر ماه و هر سال طبقه طبقه از هر قسیم و هر قوم از اطراف و جوانب بدرگاه معلی آمده بمناصب و مراتب سرفرازی می یابند و یکی از لوازم این دولت ابد پیوند آنکه هر کرا جای دیگر نباشد جای او درینجا است و هر که اینجا است بجای دیگر نرود اگر کسی را ضرورتی رود تا از حضرت خلافت رخصت حاصل ننماید بجای دیگر نمی تواند رفت و این ضابطه مخصوص (۳ب) بادشاهان عظیم الشان است بدیگری نمی رسد بنده که ازین بارگاه آسمان جاه ازلی سعادتی خود برود و پیش خود جای دهند هرگاه که قاعده چنان باشد جمعی که از روی تمام بندگی این درگاه والا اختیار نموده منصب و جاگیر یافته در سلک بندهای منتظم گشته باشند و بر ذمه بعضی ازان طلب مطالبه سرکار اعلی بوده باشد محض از روی جهالت و بی اجازت حضور راه پاپیش گیرند پدر شما و شما انهارا بپیش خود جای داده مدار علیه خود سازند و از بازپرس این معنی حذر نکنند داخل کدام خرد صواب اندیش است۔ دیگر آنکه در وقتی که مهم قندهار در میان بود هنگام امتحان عیار جوهر اخلاص بندهای عقیدت کیش بود جمعی که عدم و وجود آنها مساوی بود فرستاند در منوهر پور که قرار داد هزار سوار بود قلیلی نگاهداشتند این چه دعوی اخلاص است و پیش بادشاهان ممالک

---

[۱] در نسخهٔ دیگر۔ (ج ف ۴۰۲)۔ [۲] نسخهٔ دیگر (ج و ۴۰۲) "تا بدبنا ل داران" می دارد

ستان کوتاہی خدمت خصوصاً دریں ہنگام ضرورت تقصیر کلانست۔ چوں ایں قسم تقصیرات از جانب شما بظہور پیوست دریں وقت خاطر ملکوت ناظر اشرف اقدس اعلیٰ از ہیچ طرف نگرانی نداشت بجہت پاداش ایں جرائم عساکر ظفر طراز از اندازہ حساب افزوں و بیروں طلب داشتہ متوجہ اجمیر گردیدند و افواج قاہرہ منصورہ بر چیتور تعین فرمودند و خاصہ عزم مقدس آنکہ یا رانا بملازمت (۴۵ a) سراسر سعادت اشرف اقدس مستعد گردد یا ہرچہ بیند از خود بیند دریں اثنا فرستادہای شما رسیدند بوسیلہ باریافتگان محفل بہشت آئین استعفای تقصیرات شما نمودند و بندگان حضرت اشرف اقدس اعلیٰ بمقتضای فتوت ذاتی و مروت جبلی خانمان آبادان چندیں سالہ شمار اکہ نزدیک زوال و اختلال رسیدہ بود بحال داشتند و اکتفا بہمیں فرمودند کہ افواج قاہرہ منصورہ بقلعہ چیتور رفتہ جاہا کہ ساختہ و مرمت کردہ باشد مسمار نمودہ برگردد و پسر تیکہ در اجمیر بملازمت اشرف اعلیٰ رسیدہ سعادت ابدی حاصل نمودہ رخصت شود و جمعیت مقرری اما موجودی نہ کاغذی باشد ہمیشہ با برادران شما تعینات دکہن باشد و در آیندہ امری کہ خلاف حکم مقدس باشد از شما سر نزند در باب عنایت پرگنات نواحی اجمیر درانچہ رضای مقدس باشد بعمل خواہد آمد قدر ایں عنایت را بواقعی باید دانست و شکر ایں نعمت را بجا باید آورد و پسر تیکہ خود راز و د روانہ باید نمود و تاخیر دریں کار جایز نباید داشت۔ فقیر ایں مقدمات راست و درست و تلخ و شیریں را بشرح و بسط بزبانی و آئینی کہ در خور فرستادہای ایں دولت پایدار باشد ادا نمود۔ رانا کہ ہرگز دریں مدت گوش او آشنای ایں کلمات نشدہ بود دمی بایں تقصیرات نبردہ بمجرد استماع ایں سخناں بہوش آمد (۴۵ b) و آثار حیرت و ندامت از ناصیہ او مشاہدہ افتاد دانست کہ در درگاہ والا ایں تقصیرات عظیم بودہ است بعد ازاں یقین او شد کہ جوابی غیر از ندامت و عذر خواہی ندارد و عذر ایں تقصیرات خواست و ہمیں قدر گفت کہ اگرچہ ایں جرائم اکثر نسبت پدر من دارد و نکہ بمن اما من ہمہ را بر خود قبول دارم عذر میخواہم و امید عفو دارم بعد ازیں اصلا امری کہ خلاف مرضی مقدس باشد از من بظہور نخواہد آمد و بر جادہ بندگی زیارت از اسلاف خود ثابت قدم خواہم بود معتمدان مدار علیہ رانا کہ دریں خلوت بودند ہیچکس را جواب نیامد و پیش سخنان معقول ساکت ماندند و فقیر چوں بندہ راست و درست سرکار فیض آثار است و اصلا اغراض نفسانی مطمح نظر ندارد و پیش ایں قوم نیز از آغاز آفرینش یک گونہ اعتباری دارد مطلب

رابے حجابانہ وبے باکانہ از روی معقولیت ادا نمود۔ روز دیگر رانا درخانہ خود مشورت نمودہ پی براہ بہبود وسود خود بردہ قرار دادہ کہ پسر تیکہ خود را ہمراہ فقیر روانہ درگاہ والا نماید وسخنی کہ بعد از کنکایش بسیار برزبان آوردہ اینست کہ چون مردم درون وبیرون از رسیدن افواج قاہرہ متوہم ومضطرب شدہ اند ہمیں کہ لشکر نصرت اثر قلعہ چیتور را خراب ساختہ برگردد پسر را ہمان روز برفاقت کمترین بندگان روانہ اجمیر سازد و فقیر باو گفت کہ در فرستادن پسر واہمہ بیجا یست اظہار کرد (۵۹) کہ خاطرین بالکل جمع شدہ در فرستادن پسر سعادت میدانم اما چون اہل این دیار وحشی نہا دانند ملاحظہ کلی دارند مجبر در روانہ شدن لشکر از چیتور پسر را بلا توقف درہمان روز روانہ می سازم چون رانا و ہمراہیانش بعد از ردوبدل بسیار قرار داد این معنی نمودند عرضداشت نوشتہ مصحوب باو کہ آشنای این معاملہ است وخالی از راستی نیست فرستادند بدانچہ ظاہر میشود در فرستادن پسر سعادت میدانند اما ہمیں ملاحظہ لشکر چیتور وآمدن فوجی از جانب مندسور برآنہا مستولی شدہ آن نیز عنقریب از خاطر آنہا بری آید تا حال افواج بحر امواج بچیتور رسیدہ کاری کہ باید کردہ باشد ہمیں کہ این خبر بآنہا برسد پسر را روانہ می سازد کہ چند روز بیش از این اہل وعیال خود را باجمال واطفال بخیال فرستادہ قرار دادہ اند کہ چون لشکر ظفر اثر از چیتور برگردد انہارا باودیپور بطلبند بموجب ارشاد والا دای احکام واجب الانجام از روی راستی ودرستی نمودہ وسیر چشمی وبے غرضی خود را برانا ظاہر ساختہ وہم رانا کہ معقول تر از ارباب کنکایش خود است بحسن سلوک وسخنان راست ودرست از خود راضی گرداندہ امیدوار است کہ بکرم کریم کارساز این خدمت بوجہ احسن بتقدیم رسد ورگھناتھ سنگھ اگرچہ راجپوت است اما (۶۰) خالی از معقولیت ومعاملہ فہمی نیست درخلوت وکسرت اورا ہمہ جا با خود متفق ساختہ واو باجمعیت خود حاضر است این عرضداشت مصحوب خواجہ جمال عاقل خانی روانہ ملازمت فیض موہبت نمود اگر حرفی از وپرسیدہ شود شاید کہ درست ادا نماید۔ میوہ این ملک بالفعل ہمیں بادرنگ کلانست کہ بزبان اینجا کاکری گویند ونیشکر ہم بدنیست اناری چند از باغ رانا آوردہ بود اگرچہ سیراب بود اما شیرینی نداشت۔ میانہ روز ہوا بقدری گرم است وشبہا مائل بسردیست ورعیت این ملک جابجا فرار شدہ ابادانی کمتر در نظر می آید ودر اودیپور اثری از مہاجن وبیوپاری واہل شہر نیست وہمہ کس را نظر بر اصلاح این معاملہ است۔ ایام دولت واقبال مستدام باد۔

عرضداشت دویم نویسد - عرضداشت کمترین بندهای عقیدت کیش چندربهان زمین خدمت بلب ادب بوسیده ذره آسا بموقف عرض والا میرساند که رانا جمع ابواب ارشاد هدایت را بگوش هوش شنیده نظر برانقیاد احکام لازم الانجام اشرف اقدس ارفع اعلیٰ وبهبود حال و مال خود دانسته بسعی بندهای عقیدت کیش که تفصیل آن درحضور بعرض خواهد رسید وکنور را بعدازانقضای هفت گهڑی (۶۵) از شب شنبه رخصت نموده در نواحی اودیپور خیمه استاده کرده فرود آورده الحال سامان وهمراهیان نش میکند ورانا و معتقدان او التماسی اندامیدوارند که لشکر ظفر اثر چیتور را خراب ساخته زود برگردد که تا بخاطر جمع در اودیپور تواند بود وکنور بجمعیت خاطر باجمیر تواند رفت در کوشش از جانب بندهای تقصیر نرفته وبسخنان عقلی ونقلی پست بلند رانا را معقول ساخته شده اما چون وقت راست گفتن و درست نوشتن است انچه ازیں جماعت شنیده میشود بے کم وکاست معروضداشتن لازم است. آفتاب عالمتاب دولت واقبال تابان ودرخشان باد۔

عرضداشت سویم - عرضداشت کمترین بندهای عقیدت کیش چندربهان بعدازادای لوازم بندگی ذره وار بموقف عرض باریافتگان محفل بهشت آئین میرساند که طغرای عزای ابهت واجلال که ازدارالبرکت اجمیر شرف نفاذ یافته بود عز ورود دریافت آداب بندگی واستقبال بتقدیم رسانیده سعادت کونین حاصل نمود۔ رانا که منتظر ومترصد نوید عنایت والا بود بر مضمون عنایت مشحون آن مطلع گردیده بیشتر ازبیشتر تاکید در روانه ساختن کنور نمود۔ رانا اگرچه بعدازمشاهده منشور لامع النور ورسیدن پندهای عقیدت کیش مطمین خاطر گشته در قصد روانه ساختن (۶ سے) پسر بود اما ازغایت هیبت وهراس نظر برمراجعت لشکر فیروزی اثر داشت الحال که تبارکی بر مضمون امر لازم الاتباع که دریں وقت محض ازروی کشف صادر شده بود مطلع گردید بقوت ظاهر وباطن حاصل نمود وراه بهبود وسود خود برده معتمران وپروهتان را جمع ساخته بعدازانقضای روز جمعه بسل از گذاشتن هفت گهڑی از شب شنبه شهر محرم الحرام ساعت روانه ساختن پسر اختیار نمود چنانچه کاغذ ساعت بخط پروهتان معتمد رانا بجهت احتیاط درحضور رانا گرفته بجنس ارسال داشته ورانا اظهار می نمود که چون من سعادت اطاعت حکم بجا آورده ام یقین که به هیچ وجه من الوجوه فتوری وآسیبی بملک ومال من نخواهد رسید و زیاده ازاسلاف خود رعایت خواهم یافت و بین الاقران سربلندی حاصل

خواهم نمود و پسر من زود بمن خواهد رسید. چون صید قلوب وحشی نهاد آن کردن لازم است به بندهای درگاه دلاسا نموده خاطر او را مطمین گردانید تزلزل و تفرقه تمام بحال این ملک راه یافته بیش از رسیدن بندهای شهراودیپور خالی ساخته مال و متاع را بجوه فرستاده اند بازارها و خانها خالی افتاده اند همین نوکران رانا اندکه در شرمی باشند و مردم اینجا میگویند که اگر اصلاح این (۲۶ ب) نفرموده اند تا حال رانا در حبال بوده بتقویت و دلاسای بندهای استقلال او بحال مانده. درویشی هفتاد و پنج ساله گوشه گزین درین ملک بنظر افتاده که چهل سال است کنج خمول گرفته وقت را خوش می گذراند در نیولا شهر ویران شده تفرقه بجمعیت او نیز راه یافته از رسیدن بندهای فی الجمله امبنی بهم رسیده امابالفعل همه را دماغ بر اصلاح این معامله است. اقبال مدام باد کرد. هرداس و کلیان داس راجپوت بوقت رسیدند مجرای خدمت آنها شود.

عرضداشت چهارم. عرضداشت کمترین بندگان عقیدت نشان چندربهان برهمن پس از انجام لوازم بندگی و اخلاص ذره آسا بدروه عرض ناصیه سایان آستان عالی شان ملایک نشان میرساند که حقیقت برآمدن پسر رانا تا شب شنبه چهارم محرم از شهراودیپور و فرود آمدن خیمه که در یک کروهی از شهر نصب نموده بود داشتن رانا چشم انتظار بر معاودت لشکر فیروزی اثر قبل ازین عرضداشت نموده بود امید که بسمع والا رسیده باشد درین اثنای مشیخت و وزارت پناه شیخ عبدالکریم با فرمان مرحمت عنوان رسیده و مژده صدور حکم مراجعت لشکر نصرت اثر بگوش رانا که غیر ازین معنی در روانه ساختن پسر نداشت رسانیده (۲۷ الف) و رانا بهمان احکام سابق مطیع و منقاد گشته پسر را که گفته پیشتر از شهراودیپور برآورده بود بتازگی رهین منت و احسان و عنایت و مرحمت گردانیده شیخ مشارالیه و کمترین بندهای درگاه با پسر رانا صبح شنبه دوازدهم شهر محرم سنه بیست و هشت روانه ملازمت سعادت گردیدند خدمتی که از رسیدن بوقت که رانا از غایت اضطراب پای در رکاب و عنان در دست داشت و نگاهداشتن او بلطایف عقلی و نقلی و پست و بلند و طلبیدن پسر او از حبال و برآوردن از شهراودیپور و آمدن در زیر خیمه از بندهای با اخلاص بظهور آمده امید که بر آئینه ضمیر انور که جام جهان نما عبارت از آنست پرتو انداخته باشد. ایام دولت و اقبال دایما باد.

Chapter IV

ROYAL CHARITIES

In recounting the story of Jagat Singh and Raj Singh Ranchhod is, like other bards, very anxious to give detailed account of their generous gifts, particularly when they happened to be made to the members of his own family[86]. Weighing of Jagat Singh, his mother, Jamuvati, and Raj Singh against silver and gold is mentioned[87]. The scales that were used for weighing Jagat Singh and Raj Singh used to be pointed out with pride to all visitors to the palace at Udaipur till recently. Several other great gifts are also described under the technical names which the jurists have given them. Jagat Singh is said to have made Kalpavriksha, Svarṇaprithvi, (the earth in gold), Saptasāgara (seven oceans), Viśvachakra, Kalpalatā, Hiraṇyāśva, (goldenhorse) and Ratnadhenu gifts[88]. Raj Singh's donations are described as including Brahmāṇḍaka, Hiraṇyakāmadhenu, Mahābhūtaghaṭa, Hiraṇyāśvaratha, Kalpalatā, Panchalāngala, Saptasagara, Hemahastiratha, Hiraṇyaśva, Svarṇaprithvī, Viśvachakara, Kalpadruma, and Brahamaṇda[89]. A few of these donations are described in the text and in few other cases the cost in dams is given. Some of these gifts may have been notional only. We are told, for example, that Raj Sihgh had vowed to make a gift of an elephant to Madhusudan. Though an elephant would have cost very much more, payment of 500 silver coins squared the account[90]. An equivalent of the classical horse sacrifice is described as the giving away of a white horse with a gold saddle[91]. In some cases the money value of the gifts

86. Ranchhod V, 23 to 31.

87. Ibid, V, 32, 40, 44, VI 27; (Jambuvati); V 35, 36; (Jagat Singh, VIII, 47 XVII, 23, XVIII, 31 (Raj Singh).

88. Ibid, V, 56 to 49.

89. Ibid, VI, 32, VIII, 45, IX, 15, X, 6, 7, 20. 33, 35, XII, 29, 30, 36, 37, 38, 41, XVII, 15 to 18 XXI, 26, 27.

90. Ibid., VI, 27.

91. Ibid., VI 38, 39.

is given. A Hariṇyakāmdhenū cost Rs 2000[92]. Svarṇaprithvī involving 500 palas of gold is evaluated at Rs 28,000.[93]. This gives us the value of a pala of gold at Rs. 56 and enables us to evaluate certain other gifts mentioned in the text. Thus the Kalpalatā gift of 250 palas of gold[94] cost Rs 14000. The Viśvachakra valued at 509 pala[95] of gold was worth Rs 28000. The giving away of Kalpadruma of 200 palas[96] cost Rs 11600. The cost of certain other gifts is described in Tolas. The Hemahastīratha cost 1020 tolas of of gold[97] and the Hiraṇyāśava 80 tolas of gold[98]. Panchalāngala of 190 tolas[99] and Kalpalatā of 250 palas[100] is equated with 1028 tolas. This would make 250 palas equal to 1028 tolas, and work out at a pala equal to 3.4 tolas. Though the gifts bear classical names as in the works of the jurists like Hemadri, there is every reason to suggest that they were *equivalents* of those classical gifts rather than gifts as described by Hemadri in his *Chaturanga-Chintāmani*. Elsewhere we have the Rana using convenient equivalents. Or to put it in another form we may take it that our auothor inflates the gifts to bring them up to some classical models. Mān does not bear him out so far as the making of the precise gifts is concerned. Mān in his *Raj Vilas* makes no mention of these gifts.

The greatest gift of them all, gold Saptasāgar, given away by Raj Singh at the time of dedicating the dam in 1732 (1676), is praised highly and described but not evaluated. Seven vessels of golds were given in charity, each filled with one of the following, salt, milk, ghee, guda (brown unrefined sugar in bulk), curd, ghee mixed with sugar and water[101].

Another interesting feature of the narrative is its account

92. Ibid., VIII, 44, 45.
93. Ibid., XIV, 28.
94. Ibid., X, 33. 34.
95. Ibid., XII, 36, 37.
96. Ibid., XXI, 26.
97. Ibid., X 20, 21.
98. Ibid., XXI, 27.
99. Ibid., X, 34, 35, 36.
100. Ibid., X, 33, 34.
101. Ibid.. XVII, 9 to 29.

of marrying selected members of a princely bridegroom's party to girls selected from among the bride's side. Jagat Singh is said to have given away 27 girls in marriage, probably to members of Bhavani Singh of Bundi's party who had come to marry Jagat Singh's daughter[102]. Similarly when Raj Singh performed the marriage of his sister to prince Anup Singh Bhuratiya, seventy one other girls were given in marriage[103]. The marriage of Raj Singh's daughter Ajayakumari was accompanied by the marriage of 98 girls.[104] The Baghelas do not seem to have been generally accepted as of equal status with other Rajputs. Now that a princess of Mewar was married to a Baghela, it seems to have been considered necessary to raise their status. A very ingeneous method was selected for carrying this out. Besides other festivities, a common dinner was arranged at which Raj Singh took food in company with the Baghelas. This was thought enough to proclaim that Bhaghelas were no longer Kshatriyas of a lower rank[105].

102 Ibid., V, 29, 30.
103. Ibid., VI, 2, 3.
104. Ibid, VIII, 37 to 39.
105. Ibid, VIII, 40 to 43.
The abstract of these verses in the *Epigraphia Indica* (XXX, 102) is a little misleading. It makes the Baghelas proclaim themselves as lower in status. Ojha improves upon the text by making Ranchhod assert that the Baghelas were more meticulous in observing ritual at meals than the Sassodias of Mewar. He is here following the *Vir Vinod II*, 447, which however did not base its statement on Ranchhod. The text is clear in asserting that the difficulty arising out of (some of the) 'untouchable' relatives of Bhawani Singh was got over by Raj Singh's sitting with them. See appendix.

CHAPTER V

CONSTRUCTION OF THE DAM

The Language of the story

The story of the construction of the dam across the Gomati is the main theme of the *Rajapraśasti.* No wonder then that it runs through 13 cantos, from canto 9 to canto 21. Here again the story of the design and construction of the dam occupies only three cantos, the ninth, tenth and eleventh, while 10 cantos describe the preparations for the ceremony of the dedication, an account of the dedicatory ceremonies, the gifts and donations which were made by Raj Singh and the donations some of his guests and people in high places made at that time.

Here canto eleventh should be of special interest to students of Indian culture, particularly of Indian architecture. In describing the construction of the dam, the poet uses many architectural terms which should prove of great interest to students of Indian architecture. Among other terms, pītham, mekhalā, tilaka, sangīkārya, garbhakoshtha, sthara, koshtha, garbhakośpatha, pūrvakośatha, chatuski, kamalāburja, setushilakārya, mandapa, udayavistāra[106] are used.

Another important thing to notice is a reflection of the process of unification of the country under the Mughals. The unit of measurement used is Gaz[107], the Mughal yard. Whether it is Ilahi yard of Akbar which he used for revenue purpose or the common Gaz otherwise current is immaterial. The masons and other artisans engaged had come from far and wide and it was but natural that the measurement should be expressed in a unit current in the country at large.

But much more interesting is the Samskritization of the Persian words. No attempt seems to have been made to coin a new word for a notion which was well understood at large. Among the techical terms used Burj again is Persian word which was pressed into service without any attempt at creat-

106. Ibid, XI, 3, 4, 6, 7, 8, 9, 10, 11 etc. see Appendix.
107. Ibid, XI, 51, XII, 35.

ing a Sanskrit equivalant[108]. This tendency is a common feature of the Sanskrit works of the period. Another contemporary work, the *Sarvadeśavratāntansangraha* of Mahesh Thakur freely uses Persian and Arabic titles in Sanskrit. It also uses other Persian words to convey new notions[109].

The Project

The story of the construction of the dam must now be told. It was decided to construct a dam across the Gomti where it flowed through two big hills[110]. Two other streams Tala and Kailva, it was planned, were also to add their waters, to the reservoir that would thus be created. The sixteen villages, Dhudhunda, Sanvada, Bhimavada, Sivali, Morchana, Pasonda, Khedi, Chaprakhedika, Tasola, Medavarka, Bhana, Dupanaka, Vamsola, Godhali, Kamkroli and Matha were likely to come under water or in the the foundation of the dam. Of these Sivali, Bhimavada, Bhana, Dupanaka, and Godhali were totally submerged in the lake, while Morchana, Pasonda, Khedi, Chaparakhedika, Tasoa were partially submerged along with Mamdovara. Of the original sixteen, Dhudhunda, Sanvada, Medavarka, Vamsola and Matha seem to have escaped submergence while so far as Kankroli was concerned, its wells and tanks alone were brought under water[111].

The length of the lake is said to be 7000[112] yards. We are told that in circumscribing the lake Raj Singh walked 14 kosa[113]. This would work out at least 17.50 miles.

Such a big project could not have been easily carried out without detailed planning and supervision. The account does not give the name either of the engineer-in-chief who may have planned the whole project or of the men who carried it out. The entire credit is given to Raj Singh alone. We are told the work was divided into sections and placed

108. Ibid, XI. 7.

109. Cf. *Bibliography of Mughal India*. by Sri Ram Sharma. The work has been published.

110. Ranchod, IX, 5, 6, 13 : XII, 12.

111. Ibid, XII, 7, 8, and 9.

112. Ibid, XII, 13.

113. Ibid, XVI, 27.

under the charge of a Thakur or a Sahu. Some of these are mentioned by name in the text but the last slab (XXV) has additional matter in Marwari which mentions 20 such supervisors. Their names given in this addendum read as follows:

Maha Singh, Ram Singh, Bhao Singh, Dalapat, Mohan Singh, Lunkaran, Kesari Singh, Mohkam Singh, Narasingh Das, Garib Das, Singh, Ram Chand, Hema, Mohkam Singh Rathod Ram Chandra, Chechani, Kandu Pancholi, Rama, Mukand. Das, Har Ram Sighavi, Lashu, Maharaval Ram Singh, an uncle of the Rana, Mohan Singh and Shyamal Das seem to have been in charge of financing the work and keeping accounts[114].

The Rajasthani addendum gives the names of the chief masons as well; Bagh, Mukand, Kalyan's son, Jagannath, Megho son of Jagannath, Arjun, son of Lalo, Lasho and Jasoharji. Some of them have been mentioned earlier in similar addenda at the end of some of the cantos, Mukand, Jagan Nath, Lalo, Lasho, Jasoharji and Meghomani. The names of two Sutradhaṛs—master masons—Mohan and Sushji are also mentioned here. Earlier addenda add the names of Arjun, Sukhdev[116], Keso, Sunder, Lalaji[115], Kalyan's son Ram Nath[117]. Two lables are used for chief artisans working on the project, some are designated, Gajādhara, wielder of the gaj, the measuring yard, others as Sutradhara, wielder of the measuring string.

The list of the chief artisans and artists is short but we learn elsewhere that as many as 60,000 workmen were sometimes employed on the project[118]. No wonder that the total wage bill came to Rs 32,02,880[119]. It is interesting to compare this with what has been supposed to be the Mughal practice in erecting their magnificient forts, gardens, palaces

114. Ibid, XX, 31. The inscription counts it as verse 29, there being two verses numbered 28. XXI, 3 to 9.

115. Ibid, at the end of canto II.

116. Ibid, at the end of canto V.

117. Ibid, at the end of canto VII.

118. Ibid, IX, 17.

119. Ibid, XXI, 12, 13.

and tombs where it is suggested that forced labour on payment of board only was employed.

Progress of the Work

The first and a very tough job was to drain off the river to get to dry bed on which foundations for the dam could be laid. Many devices were used for the purpose. The mahurta for beginning the work was performed on 1 January, 1662[120]. It took three years before the foundations of the dam could be laid in the bed of the river. Ranchhod, son of Purohita Gharib Das, laid the foundations on 17 April, 1665[121].

By February 1669 the Rana had a palace built for him on the banks of the river where the present city of Raj Nagar stands. Its housewarming ceremony was performed with due rituals[122] on 8 December, 1669.

By May, the position of the dam adjacent to the town of Kankroli had been completed. Its mahurta was now performed on 11 May, 1670[123].

When the rains set in, the newly created artificial lake started filling in. By 26 June, 1670 the main dam was ready after a labour of eight years, five months and six days according to the Hindu reckoning[124].

The main dam being now complete, the ornamental work on the lake was started, Square foundations had been dug deep in the bed at different places for constructing square pleasure resorts inside the lake[125].

The lake was now filling up with water which rose so as to allow the launching of boats. It was now decided to launch the first boat in the lake. A day before the launching ceremony there was not enough water to allow a boat to be well and truely launched. Much anxiety was felt, running even to dismay, as another suspicious day for the purpose

120. Ibid, IX, 14.
121. Ibid, IX, 34.
122. Ibid, X 1 to 5.
123. Ibid, X, 10.
124. Ibid, X, 12, 13.
125. Ibid, X, 16, 17 and 18.

was not available for more than a year thereafter. Much anxious thought was given to the problem of bringing enough water into the excavated area. Purohita Gharib Das had a brain wave. The recitation of the *Varuna* hymns was started immediately in order to persuade a propitiated Indra, lord of rain, to send rain. As it happened, it rained heavily in the afternoon. Rana Raj Singh was able to perform the ceremony on the appointed day, 26 June, 1670, with great pomp and show[126].

By May, 1672 the construction had become strong enough on all sides to stand the pressure of water. All outlets of water from the lake were now closed. On 6 March 1673 the Rana performed the muhurta of the Samgikārya of the dam and felt very happy on its being well accomplished by clever masons[127].

Shipwrights sent for from Lahore, Gujarat and Surat got busy constructing a very big boat, almost a ship—Jahaj. Water was now rising fast in the lake. By August, 1674 it was so deep that the *Jahaj* could now be safely launched. The ship builders were successful in launching one on 25 August, 1674 and thus establish the capacity of the lake for big 'ships' as well[128]. The dam was now complete, the lake full of water. Tradition required that it be duly dedicated. An auspicious day had to be fixed for the ceremony. The astrologers found 15 January, 1576 as a fitting day for such a solemn undertaking[129].

It was a great achievement, probably the greatest work of public utility constructed by any ruler in medieval India. The total cost already incurred amounted to well above Rs 30 lakhs. When further works were completed by 1679, it had run into Rs, 39,32,002.

The Dam

The dam forms an irregular segment of a circle, em-

126. Ibid, X, 22 to 32.

127. Ibid, XII, 35, 36.

128. Ibid, XIII, 38. The verse in the inscription is wrongly numbered as 50.

129. Ibid, X, 37, 38, 39.

bracing an extent of nearly three miles and encircling the northest and north—east points. The barrier confines a sheet of water about twelve miles in circumference and is entirely of white marble, with a flight of steps of the same material, throughout this extent from the summit to the water's edge.

APPENDIX

Architectural Terms used

भूम्यर्द्धम् । पीठम् ।। Verse 3

मेखला तिलक: ।। Verse 4

संगिकार्य: । स्थरम् ।।। Verse 5

बुरिज । Verse 7

कमल बुरिज । Verse 54

कोष्ठं ।। Verse 7

गर्भकोष्ठं ।। Verse 9

पूर्वकोष्ठं ।। Verse 10

मध्यकोष्ठं Verse 50

अन्त:कोष्ठं Verse 49

सेतु: ।। Verse ।

सोपानमाला । Verse 13

अरहट्टकम् Verse 16

चतुष्की ।। Verse 17

मंडप । सेतुमंडप ।। Verse 51

VI

THE CONSECRATION CEREMONY OF THE RAJSAMUND

The Dedication Ceremony

The dedication ceremony of the lake had to fit the large amount spent on its construction and the great utility that the work held out for irrigational purposes. Nine cantos from the thirteenth to the twenty first are mainly devoted to a description of the ceremonies connected with the dedication, gifts made by Rana Raj Singh and a description of the dam, other constructions and the total expenditure.

Raj Singh now sent invitations far and wide to rulers, thakurs, relatives, friends, learned men, poets, charans (bards) and men of piety[130].

The celebrations seem to have begun early in January. Three *mandapas* were set up on the dam, one for the dedication ceremony, one for weighing the Rana against gold, and a third one for the giving away of Hataka saptasagar gift. These were tastefully decorated, with beautiful pillars, keeping the mandaps open on all the four sides[131].

Appointment of various priests

On 10 January on the advice of the Raj Purohita Gharib Das the Rana appointed, as laid down in the *Matsya Purana*, 26 'Ritvigs' (priests) for the performance of the ceremonies; one Brahma (presiding director), one Acharya (presiding priest), 8 Japakas, reciters of verses and 8 keepers of the gates and 8 Hotris (priests pouring in libations into the sacred fire).[132]

Tula Dana

The Rana now announced that he would have himself

130. Ibid, XIII, 21, 22, The verses are wrongly numbered 22 and 23 in the inscription. The verse after the tenth has been wrongly numbered twelfth.

131. Ibid, XIII, 30 (wrongly numbered 41 in the inscription).

132. Ibid, XIII, 41, The inscription makes them verses 51 and 52 by first missing verse eleven and then jumping from verse 23 to 34.

weighed against gold and give away the amount in charity. This caught on. Soon there were other claimants for this honour and several other Mandaps had to be constructed for the purpose. Purohita Gharib Das had announeed that he would have himself weighed against gold, his son against silver. The Rani of Toda, whose husband was an uncle of the Rana, Rao Kesari Singh of Solambar and Barhatt Kesari Singh similarly announced their desire to get themselves weighed against silcer[133].

Propitiatory rites

On the 14 January 1676 Raj Singh entered the Mandap set up for the main ceremony. He had earlier gone through a purificatory penance. After the chanting of the hymns invoking blessing for the enterprise, he worshipped the godess Dharitri (earth), Ganesh (harbinger of happiness), Gotradevi, (goddess of the clan) and Govind. The priests then duly entered upon their duties and were, as such, offered preliminary offerings. The Rana then washed their feet.[134] Thereafter the regular preliminary ceremonies for the dedication of the lake began. The god of ocean, Varuna. was now propitiated[134]. This was followed by a Jala-Yatra when the Rana went in a procession accompanied by priests, with ladies carrying pitchers full of water from the lake. After marching through the city the procession ended at the mandapa prepared for the purpose. Here the ladies unloaded their pitchers which were tastefully arranged in rows. The Rana now propitiated the nine heavenly bodies, paid homage to Varuna, and propitiated Rudra in order to ensure happiness and prosperity in his land[135].

The Rana spent the night in the mandapa along with others who were to take part in the Mahurta ceremony next morning[136].

Early on the morning of 15 January the Rana entered the main mandap accompanied by his relatives, including

133. Ibid, XIV. 1 to 10.
134. Ibid, XIV, 14 to 40.
135. Ibid, XV, 1 to 15.
136. Ibid, XV, 16.

the ladies[136]. In company with his chief Rani, he performed the worship of Varuna which, the poet declares, is equivalent to the worship of all the other gods put together. In order to make this lake another Ratnakara (ocean), the Rana now threw in nine precious stones, fish and tortoises. The poet tells us the alligators were also thrown in. It is difficult to believe that they were first captured somewhere, brought to Raj Nagar and then thrown into the lake. The Rana now worshipped a cow with a calf. Then followed the ceremony of Gotaran with a view to win victory in war and the destruction of the enemies[138].

Naming the new lake

Now arose the question of fixing a name for the lake. Rajasagar and Rojasamundra were the two names suggested. The Rana accepted both the names. An auspicious day was now fixed when the naming ceremony was performed on 20 January 1677[139].

The ceremony of the Parikrama

One of the most colourful ceremonies was yet to come. The Rana had to go round the lake before it could be named and dedicated. Rana Udai Singh had gone round Udai Sagar in a palanquin. Raj Singh however decided to do better. He decided to walk round the lake and walk barefooted at that. To begin with the entire retinu had to accompany the king on foot. But the Rana had mercy on some of his companions and allowed the chief Rani and his brother to get into palanquins.

The 14 'koses' of the circumference took six days to complete. The Rana's progress was slow. Charities were being given away on the way, flower garlands being offered and accepted. So by five easy marches the Rana completed the ceremony[140]. He must have began the 'parikrama' on 15 January and completed it on 20 January to be back in the mandap for the final naming and dedicatory ceremonies on 20 January.

137. Ibid, XV 16.
138. Ibid,XV, 21 to 30.
139. Ibid. XVI 28.
140. Ibid. XVI 2 to

Dedication ceremony, donations and gifts

On 20th January the naming ceremony of the lake and the final dedicatory rites were performed. The sacrifice over, the naming done, after the last oblation had been offered to the sacred fire, the lake stood dedicated for public good.

In the sacrificial pavilion the Rana was accompanied by his brother Arsi, his sons Jai Singh, Bhim Singh, Gaj Singh Surjan Singh, Indra Singh and Bahadur Singh, his grandsons, the Raja purohita, Gharib Das, the Diwan, Bhika, and various other princes and thakurs.

The gold 'Saptasāgara' donation was now given away. The Rana was weighed against gold with his grandson Amar Singh in his lap. Nine thousand tolas of gold, worth the weight of the two were given away in charity. This was followed by similar Tula dans by the chief Rani, Sadakumari who was weighed against silver. Gharib Das had himself weighed against gold, his son Ranchhod, Rao Kesari Singh Chohan, Barhat Kesari Singh and an aunt of the Rana all were weighed againt silver.[141]

All this, and much more, was distributed among the 46000 Brahamans who wera present on the occasion. Gifts were also distributed among other guests as well.[142] This over, missions bearing gifts were despatched to Raja Jaswant Singh of Jodhpur, Raja Ram Singh of Jaipur, Rao Anup Singh of Bikaner, Rao Bhavani Singh of Bundi, Rao Mukand Das of Rampur, Raval Amar Singh of Jaisalmer, Rao Jaswent Singh of Dungarpur and Raja Bhavani Singh of Rewa.[141] Among those present on the occasion, the Diwan Bhika, Maharavala Ram Singh, who was the supervisor in-chief of the work and Rana's aunt of Toda received substntial gifts. Bards and several other thakurs were also not forgotten.[142]

141. Ibid, XVI, 34 to 40; XVII, 25 to 30 XVIII 1 to 15. The weight of the Rana and his grandson together, of 9000 Tolas as in the text works at 2 maunds and 22 1/2 seers. The grandson was less than three years old.

142. Ibid, XIX, 23.

143. Ibid, XX, 1 to 26.

144. Ibid, XX, 29 to 43.

A very interesting piece of information the narrative gives us is a list of the rulers of Chitor whose grants some minstrels and bards were still enjoying. The list occurs in an account of the gifts made on the last day. We have grantees of Jagat Singh, Karan Singh, Amar Singh, Pratap, Udai Singh, Vikram, Ratansi, Samgram Singh, Rai Mal, Kheta, Ajesi and Samarsi.[145] We can rely on the accuracy of the bard here as he gives detailed figures of the gifts which each class of grantees recived. This would establsh a line of succession in Mewar which one could rely on. This list puts Lekha (Lakshman Singh), Kheta and Ajesi between Samarsi and Hamir[146] and contradicts the list of rulers given elsewhere in the narrative. It differs from other lists so far known from several inscriptions. Raval Salivahan has also been put in between Ajesi and Samarsi but given the specific title Raval to distinguish him from the rest. Ari Singh and Kshem Singh of the Mount Abu inscription of Vikram era 1342[147] may be our Ajesi and Lekha.

145. Ibid, XX, verses 44 to 51. The verses are wrongly numbered in the inscription 40 to 47.

146. Ibid, XX, 50 (wrongly numbered 46 in the inscription).

147. *Indian Antiquary*, XVI, 347.

Chapter VII

AURANGZEB AND MARWAR

Jaswant Sing's death

The Rajput war had its origins in Aurangzeb's attempt at capturing Jodhpur after Raja Jaswant Singh's death in December, 1678, three years after the consceration ceremony of the Rajasamund. It is well to remember that the construction work at the dam went on after the dedication ceremony was completed in 1735 A.V. (1679).[148] The incidents mentioned about the war therefore would be the nearest to the time of the composition of the work. That would not, by itself, be reason enough for our story to be entirely trustworthy. Poets are poor historians, men of letters learn little of the affairs of the state. As we shall soon see even this part of the narrative is neither entirely straight, nor entirely trustworthy.

Before we take up the story of the Mewar-Mughal conflict as told by our author, it is necessary to relate certain other facts with which Ranchhod has not concerned himself.

Maharaja Jaswant Singh in 1678 was the premier Hindu noble holding the rank of a Haft Hazari (a 7000er, to use Morerland's method of describing Mughal ranks). To meet the Afghan danger he had been stationed as the independent commander of the Mughal garrisson at Jamrud guarding the Kheyber pass. It is true that he was not the governor of Kabul as Sir Johnat Sarkar asserted sneeringly.[149] He was a thanadar certainly, but an independent thanadar. The Mughal governor of the province, Amir Khan did not hold as high a rank as he did. Ths command of this garrisson was a post of honour. We find it described as involving the patrolling and safeguarding of the way through Khybar pass from Jamrud to Haft Jah when it was conferred on Ram Singh of Jaipur in 1681.[150] In 1683 while occupying this

148. Ranchhod, XXI, 1.

149. *Aurangzeb*, vol III, 325, note.

150. *Jaipur Records* (MS), Volume III, 48, 66, 135.

post Ram Singh was required to render help to all officers from Peshawar to Attock.

Jaswant Singh died on 28 December, 1678[151]. Aurangzeb received the news of his death at Jamrud from his news-writer at Peshawar. Aurangzeb thereupon orderd Raja's confident, Durga Dass, to bring the Raja's family to Delhi. Durga Das Rathor, Sonak, Raghu Nath Das Bhatt, and Ranchhod, among others, thereupon, set out for Delhi on 14 January, 1679 with the Maharaja's family.

Posthumous Birth of Two sons

When the party reached Lahore, two of the widowed Ranis gave birth to two sons on 19 February, 1679[152]. Aurangzeb heard the news of their birth when he was at Ajmer on 26 February, 1679. After staying for some time in Lahore, the Rajputs resumed their march to Delhi. One of the sons died on the way. In Delhi the entire party put up at the Jodhpur palace in Jaswant Pura. Durga Das as the leader of the party now approached Aurangzeb and requested that the infant be recognised as Jaswant Singh's successor in Jodhpur.[153] Aurangzeb, however, placed guards all round the palace. Durga Das was still not downhearted. The late Maharaja had many friends among the Muslim officials. Durga Das now sought the intervention of Hassan Quli Khan who had just returned to Delhi from Jodhpur after putting down local disturbances there. He presented the Rathor delegation at the imperial court. They once again requested Aurangzeb to bestow Jodhpur on Ajit. Aurangzeb would have none of it. Enraged at a Mughal commander's daring to intervene on behalf of the Rathors Aurangzeb dismissed him from office[154].

151. Basātin-i-Salātīn, 516, and Maāsar 'Ālamīrī, 173, put the date at 10 December, 1678. But Jodhpur tradition however puts the date of his death as 10 Paush Badi, 1735 on Thursday which is equivalent to 28 December, 1678. It is curious that Rau who cites this traditon (241) equates the Hindi date with 28 November. Jaswant Singh's death on 28 December above explains the Rathor's leaving Jamrud as late as 14 January, 1678. Rau has cited *Rājarūpaka* as his authority which he reproduces in original.

152. Rau, 248.

153. *Maāsir-i-Ālamgīrī*, 171, 172.

154. Ibid, 172 to 177; *Fatuhāt-i-Ālamgiri*. (Ms), 72, 73, to 75 a.

Aurangzeb's Moves after Jaswant Singh's Death

Jaswant Singh's death without a son and heir had raised delicate questions of imperial rights in the state. The Mughul theory held that every Rajput ruler ruled even over his own hereditary territory as a grant from the Mughal emperor. As some of Rajas rose in imperial command, they were given additional territories as well. A distinction was made between the Watan (his own territory) Jagir and the additions made thereto. As a commander of 7000 Maharaja Jaswant Singh had held additional areas as well outside Jodhpur. At his death these naturally reverted to the emperor.

But there was Jodhpur proper to be dealt with. According to Hindu law and Rajput custom, Ajit became Jaswant Singh's successor as soon as he was born. But Rajput Rajas had occassionally used the fiction of the imperial grant regulating succession to change the line of succession. Jaswant Singh himself was not the eldest son of his father. His elder brother, Amar Singh was alive elsewhere when Jaswant Singh succeeded his father at Jodhpur. Earlier in Jodhpur's history, a sixth son had been exalted to the gaddi at his father's wishes but with previous imperial confirmation[156]. Here Aurangzeb found a situation wherein he could manuvour enough. Jaswant Singh had no heir of his body at the time of his death. Aurangzeb could assert that this left the entire question to his diseretion. Of course no Rajput State had earlier faced such a situation during the Mughal rule. No Rajput ruler could have ever dreamt that his State could be resumed by the emperor[157]. Aurangzeb therefore decided to move cautiously, though firmly.

Immediately on hearing the news of Jaswant Singh's death he appointed his own officers at Jodhpur. On 13 January, 1679 Tahawar Khan was named Fojdar (head of the administration) of Jodhpur, Khidmat Guzar Khan had been appointed the garrison commander and Shaikh Anwar, treasurer and Abdur Rahim, kotwal of Jodhpur[158]. Aurangzeb

156. Cf *Studies in Medieval Indian History* by Sri Ram Sharma, 197 to 206.

157. Cf. Ibid.

158. *Maasir-Alamgiri*, 171.

then started for Ajmer and reached there on 19 February 1672—the day the Rathor Rani gave birth to two sons—to be near enough Jodhpur for any eventualities. Before he had reached Ajmer he had told off a royal army for the purpose of proceeding against Rathors in Jodhpur with the Khan Jahan as its head[159].

Jai Singh at the Mughal Court

Aurangzeb's attempt at sequestering Jodhpur went without protest outside Jodhpur. While he was at Ajmer, a letter from the Rana is said to have been received in which it was alleged, he proposed to send his son, Jai Singh, to the court. On 8 March a royal order was issued assigning Muhammad Naim to the task of going to Udaipur and bring Jai Singh to the imperial presence.[160] Our author tells us[161] that Raj Singh sent Jai Singh on 10 Chaitra (bright half), 1735 to the Mughal court. As we learn a little later, Purohita Gharib Das, Jhala Chander Sen and several other thakurs accompanied him on his mission.[162] Our author does not mention Naim but he must have been one of the party as the emperor had told him off for this duty earlier. When Jai Singh reached Ajmer the party found that Auranzeb had already left for Delhi on 30 March. Naturally the party moved on to Delhi. Two koses on the Ajmer side of Delhi, Jai Singh caught up with the Mughal party.

To show Jai Sigh honour, Indar Singh, son of Raj Singh was now deputed to lead Jai Singh to the imperial presence. He was presented to Aurangzeh on 11 April, 1679.,[163] and was lavishly rewarded by a string of pearls, gold ornaments, an elephant, a bolt of brocade and horses. Gharib Das and Jhala Chander Sen and other Rajput dignitaries accompanylng the prince were also suitably honoured.[164]

159. *Fatuhat-i-Alamgiri* 73 a, *Maasir-i-Alamgiri*, 172.

160. Correspondence preserved in Udaipur Archives and reproduced in the *Vir Vinod*, II, 457 to 459.

161. Ranchhod, XXII, 1 and 2, G. N. Sharma in his *Mewar and Mughal Emperors*, 163 wrongly asserts that Jai Singh left Udaipur after the imposition of the Jizya on 1 April. *Maasir-i-Alamgiri* (173) wrongly dates sending of Muhammad Naim at 10 March.

162. Ranchhod XX II, 6.

163 *Maasir-i-Alamgiri*, 173.

164. Ranchhod, XXII, 5, 6.

Jai Singh remained in Delhi for about 3 weeks and was given leave to depart on 29 April.[165] He made pilgrimage to Garh Muktesar, Mathura and Bindraban[166] and returned to Udaipur in June, 1679.[167]

Meanwhile on 12 April, Aurangzeb had reimposed the hateful Jizya on all non-Muslims throughout the empire. Jai Singh must have learnt of the protest which the Hindus of Delhi staged when Aurangzeb went to say his Friday prayers in the mosque in Delhi, the Friday after the imposition.[168]

On returning home, the Udaipur officials must have informed the Rana all that they might have seen or heard about Aurangzeb's designs against the Hindus. The Rana could have hardly been expected to swallow Aurangzeb's attempt at levying Jizya in Udaipur. He is said to have addressed a letter of protest to the emperor.[169] But events at Delhi were moving too fast to leave the Rana much time to make up his mind on this score.

Unrest at Jodhpur

After Jaswant Singh's death there had been disturbance in Jodhpur. Dhiraj and Harji had been reported to be stirring up trouble in Jodhpur and on 7 February, 1679 Aurangzeb had detailed Khan-i-Jahan and Hasan Quli Khan to proceed to Jodhpur and occupy it. Aurangzeb left Ajmer on 10th March to reach Delhi on 12 April.[170] He had learnt on 9 March that Khan Jahan had been able to occupy Jodhpur without much serious resistance. He had appointed his own commanders at various

165. *Maasir-i-Alamgiri*, 173.

166. Ranchhod, XXII, 6 to 9.

167. Ibid, XXII, 9. Ojha (II, 5 and 6) wrongly dates the return on 15 May. Rather surprisingly he gives the Hindu equivalent at Jaist Shudi 1,1736 on the authority of Ranchhod which it is difficult to under stand. Ranchhod does not give a date. He only mentions the month of Jaiyashth.

168. Mamuri, 525, 526. On the imposition and collection of Jizya, Cf the *Religious Policy of the Mughal Emperors* by Sri Ram Sharma.

169. See Appendix.

170. Ishar Das 73; *Maasir-i-Alamgiri.*, 172.

important places in Marwar,. and had taken possession of all the property of Jaswant Singh. Anayat Khan was sent to Jodhpur to carry out imperial orders and assess the revenues of Jodhpur. Aurangzeb was informed the same day that Khidmat Guzar Khan, the commander of the fort in Jodhpur, had failed to find the State treasury in the fort of Shivanah. Abdur Karim was now sent to dig in the fort for treasure.[171]

Appointment of Indar Singh

On 25 May, 1679 Khan Jahan returned from Jodhpur to Delhi. He had shown a crusader's zeal in Jodhpur. He had destroyed several temples there and as a witness to his religious zeal brought back cartloads of idols in brass, stone, silver, gold and some studded with precious stones.[172] But Aurangzeb does not seem to have been sure that he would be able to keep Jodhpur for long under imperial control. Now that there was a Rathor claimant to the throne in the person of infant Ajit Singh, Aurangzeb decided to retrace his steps and conferred the government of Jodhpur, on Indar Singh, a grand nephew of Jaswant Singh and grand son of his elder brother Amar Singh who had been disinherited. Indar Singh held Nagore as a Jagir. On 26 May, 1679 Indar Singh was proclaimed the ruler of Jodhpur in succession to Jaswant Singh. This was not a makeshift arrangement nor an improvization to keep out Ajit. The happy recipient of the honour, Indar Singh, paid Rs. 36 lacs as a Nazr to the emperor on his being nominated the Raja of Jodhpur.[173] He left for Jodhpur now via Nagoer. The Rathor chiefs at Jodhpur left him alone for the time being. The Marwar tadition has it that he partly succeeded in winning over some of the Marwar Chiefs.[174]

Thus when Durga Das and other Rathors demanded justice on behalf of Ajit, Aurangzeb stood committed other-

171. *Court Bulletins* of 9 March, 1679.
172. *Maasir-i-Alamgiri*, 175, 176.
173. Ishar Das, 75 a, *Maasir-i-Alamgiri*, 175.
Mewar and the Mughal Emperors wrongly assert that this was a stop gap arrangement. Indar Singh paid a Peshkash of Rs. 36 lacs. It could be argued that he had as good a title to Jodhpur as the infant Ajit.

174. Rau, I. 253.

wise. He could not now easily recognize Ajit as Jaswant Singh's successor as he had already nominated Indar Singh to that status.

The Rathor had to decide in a hurry what to do now. They left Jaswant Singh's palace and moved into Raja Rai Singh's house where they probably thought themselves safer. Aurangzeb now ordered that Ajit be surrendered to him so that he be brought up in the royal palace. It was declared that on reaching maturity he would receive royal favours. For the maintenance of Ajit Singh two mahals (districts) were to be assigned to him but they were to be managed by the imperial adminstrators.[175] It is difficult to understand why Aurangzeb was anxious that Ajit be surrendered to him. Of course there was no love lost between Indar Singh and followers of Jaswant Singh. With or without Ajit Singh in Jodhpur, Rathors would not have tamely allowed Indar Singh to exercise authority in the State. Unless Aurangzeb intended disqualifying Ajit Singh for his claim on the throne by converting him to Islam—and one historian alleges that such were his intentions.[176]—a captive Ajit Singh was not of much use to him. As events soon proved he was clearly mistaken if he believed that the Rathors would surrender Ajit Singh easily.

On receiving the imperial orders Durga Das held a consultation with other Rajputs. Raghu Nath Bhatt and Ranchhod Jodhavat now declared that, may what happen, Ajit should not be surrendered to the Emperor. No one could be sure what Aurangzeb in his wrath might do to Ajit Singh, they asserted. The party decided to take Ajit Singh and the Maharaja's family to Jodhpur even at the cost of their lives.

Aurangzeb was now informed that the baby prince could not be separated from his mother. When he grew up it was promised, he would present himself at the court[177].

175. Ishar Das, 75 a ; *Bnsatin-i Salatain*, 517.
176. *Nuskha-i-Dilkussha*, 165, 166.
177. Ishar Das, 75 a and b; 76 a, *Massir-i-Alamgiri*, 177, 178.

On this Aurangzeb ordered on 15 July that the child be removed to Nurgarh House and the Rajputs prevented from proceeding towards Jodhpur. Several officers were deputed to carry out these orders. The Mughal officers tried to persuade the Rathors to hand over Ajit Singh but the Rajputs would have none of it. The house was now surrounded on all sides by the Mughal army. An engagement followed in which fire-arms were freely used on both sides. The Rathors soon realized that they would be overpowered.[178] The Mughal contingent was very large. Its losses could be immediately made up by new replacements, whereas the thinning out of the Rathor ranks was beyond repair. Raghu Nath now suggested to Durga Das that he should escape to Marwar with the Maharaja's family. Raghu Nath undertook to cover their flight by rearguard action. To carry through the plan Raghu Nath sallied forth at the head of one hundred soldiers to give battle to the Mughals. When the Mughals engaged his band of brave warriors, Durga Das slipped out with Ajit and Jaswant Singh's Ranis in male attire. Raghu Nath kept the Mughals engaged for more than an hour and a half. Seventy of his men lay dead on the field.

Meanwhile Mughals had discovered the ruse. Another party under Hamid Khan gave chase to Durga Das and came up with him when he had covered about 6 miles. Here Ranchhod at the head of one hundred soldiers eame up to meet the Mughals, allowing Durga Das to escape safely with Ajit. It was thought extremely dangerous to keep the Ranis in the party. In the interest of the young prince they now put an end to their lives so that Durga Das may run away without any worry for their safety. Ranchhod fought a rearguard action detaining the Mughals there for four gharis. When 60 of his Rajputs had been killed, the Mughals were able to proceed further on the road. After going about 4 miles or so, the Mughals again caught up with Durga Das's party. Another fifty Rajputs under Durga Das now blocked the Mughal advance, while Ajit

178. Ishar Das, 76 a and b, *Maasir-i-Alamgiri*, 178, 179. *Basatini Salatin*, 516.

was spirited away by a party of 40 Rajputs. The Mughals thought that Ajit would be somewhere with Durga Das and fought hard against the Rathors. He was able to keep the Mughals engaged for an hour or so when on being wounded dangerously, he made a feint and slipped away with seven soldiers, Night was now falling and the Mughal party returned to Delhi empty-handed. Of course the Rathors lost most of their belongings. A part of it was plundered, the rest was deposited in the imperial treasury. The dead bodies of both the Ranis and of Ranchhod were in-dentified where they lay dead along with 30 Rajputs.[179] Durga Das now hurried to Marwar and reached Jodhpur on 23 July, 1679.

A new Ajit Acknowledged

Meanwhile In Delhi Aurangzeb was very much upset at this successful defiance of Mughal authority in the imperial capital. To appease the emperor, Folad Khan, Kotwal of Delhi, presented an infant at court whom, he said, he had recovered from the house of a milkman where the Rathors were alleged to have left him. Some of the housemaids of the widowed Ranis had also been left behind. They now gave Aurangzeb the welcome assurances that the infant was Ajit Singh. Aurangzeb proclaimed him Jaswant's son and entrusted him to the household of Zeh-un Nissa. The next day the Kotwal followed up his discovery of the infant by producing his ornaments and other belongings. Aurangzeb now proclaimed the infant whom Durga Das had spirited away 'an imposter'.

Mamuri tells us that in order to befool the Mughals, Durga Das had a peasant's son dressed in princely clothes. The Rathors left him in a milkman's house along with two females who were similarly attired[180]. It must have been this infant whom Folad Khan had presented at court. But this was not enough. Durga Das had defied Aurangzeb in his imperial capital. But still more galling was the news received at court in July. It was reported

179. *Raj Vilas*. VI. 101 to 106.
180. *Maasir-i-Alamgiri*, 178; Mamuri (in Khafi Khan) II, 259; Bhim Sen, 164, 165; *Ajitodava*, VI, 91,93; *Rajarupaka*, 11, *Kalimati-i-Tavybai*, 30a.

that even before Ajit had reached Jodhpur, Rai Singh. Rathor had collected a very large army—*Massir-i-Alamgiri* would have it as beyond count—and attacked Ajmer. Tahawar Khan, the Fojdar, gave battle which continued raging furiously for three days. A large number of soldiers were killed on both sides. The death of Rai Singh in battle made it possible for the imperialists to claim it a victory for the Mughal army. Aurangzeb was enraged when he learnt that the Rathors had struck at the imperial territories. Aurangzeb sent a strong army under Sar Baland Khan on 17 August, 1679 to Jodhpur. He was instructed to capture Jaswant Singh's family and bring them to Delhi alive. Durga Das was to be driven out of Jodhpur and killed. For his incapacity to keep peace in Jodhpur, Tahawar Khan who had been appointed administrator of Jodhpur was dismissed from office and lost his title of Khan. Indar Singh's appoint-hoped to ment had also now lost all meaning. How Aurangzeb had reconcile the existence of a Mughal fojdar and a Rathor Raja at Jodhpur, it is difficult to understand. As long as the eyesore of a Mughal administrator remained in office at Jodhpur, Indar Singh's presence could have served no purpose. To leave the field free for the new commander, he was also recalled[181].

Of all this our author mentions nothing. But Aurangzeb's moving to Ajmer to guide operations in Rajputana after Ajmer had been threatened finds metion in our record. Aurangzeb, Ranchhod tell us, entered Mewar on 11 Paush (dark) 1736, 2 January, 1680[182]. Persian records tell us that Aurangzeb reached Ajmer on 25 September, 1679[183].

On the authority of the news letters of Ajmer for the years 1679 and 1680 it has been suggeaued that Rathors in Jodhpur were so much in love with their 'country' that proposals were made on behalf of the Haḍa Rani—Jaswant

181. *Maasir-i-Alamgiri*, 179, 180, Ishar Das, 76 b, Bhim Sen, 165, Indar Singh was only recalled to court but not 'dethroned' from his position as the Rana of Jodhpur as Sarkar has asserted (Aurangzeb, I, 334), He was appointed Thanader of Nimach later on.

182. Ranchhod, XXII, 9.

183. *Maasir-i-Alamgiri*, 180,181.

Singh's widow resident at Jodhpur whne he died—and the Rathor leader Sonak that if the emperor would keep Indar Singh out of Jodhpur, the Rathors were prepared to demolish all temples at Jodhdur and promulgate the Muslim law in the State.[183a] Naturally Aurangzeb did not take the offer seriously, it could not have been made in earnest. It is difficult to believe that such an offer, if ever made, was meant to be kept. It has further been suggested that the Rathors would have preferred the State to be incorporated in the Khalsa, rather than accept Indar Singh![183b] Indar Singh was appointed to Jodhpur after Ajit was born and a claim had been put forward on his behalf, the offer, if ever made, does not prove that the Rathors had ever liked to be governed as a province of the empire ! Jodhpur had been kept Khalsa for five months but only as a temporary measure, the Rathors may have argued that another period of Khalsa administration could easily be followed by the recognition of Ajit's claim in time. Indar Singh's installation seemed to imply permanent rejection of Ajit's claim.

183a. *Waqiat-i-Ajmtr*, 944.
183b. Ibid, 244.

APPENDIX

Raj Singh's Alleged Letter to Aurangzeb.

'All due praise be to the glory of the almighty and the munificence of your majesty which is conspicuous as the sun and the moon. Although I, your well wisher, have separated myself from your presence, I am nevertheless zealous in the performance of every bound act of obedience and loyalty. My ardent wishes and strenuous services are employed to promote the kings, nobles, mirzas, and rais of the provinces of Hindustan and chiefs of Iran, Turan, Room, and Sham, the inhabitants of seven climates, and all persons travelling by land and by water. This my inclination is notorious, your royal wisdom cannot entertain a doubt thereof. Reflecting, therefore, on my former services and your majesty's condescension, I presume to solicit the royal attention to some circumstances in which the public as well as private welfare is greatly interested.

'I have been informed that enormous sums have been dissipated in the prosecution of the designs formed against me, your well wisher, and that you have ordered Jizya to be levied to satisfy the exigencies of your exhausted treasury.

'May it please your majesty, your royal ancestor Muhammad Jalal-ud Din Akbar, whose throne is now in heaven, conducted the affairs of this empire in equity and firm security for the space of fifty two (?) years, preserving every tribe of men in care and happiness, whether they were followers of Jesus, or of Moses, of David or Muhammad, whether they were Brahman, or of the sect of Dehrias which denies the eternity of matter, or that which attributes the existence of the world to chance; they all equally enjoyed his countenance and favour, in so much that his people in gratitude for equal protection he afforded them, distinguished him by the appellation of Jagadgurn.

'His majesty Muhammad Nurud Din Jahangir, likewise, whose dwelling is now in paradise, extended for twenty two years the shadow of his protection over the heads of his people, successful by constant fidelity to his allies and a vigorous exertion of his arm in business.

'Nor less did the illustrious Shah Jahan, by a propitious reign of thirty two years, acquired to himself immortal reputation, the glorious reward of clemency and virtue.

'Such were the benevolent inclinations of your ancestors. While they pursued these great and generous principles, wheresoever they directed their steps, conquest and prosperity went before them, and then they reduced many countries and fortresses to their obedience. During your majesty's reign, many have been alienated from the empire, and further loss of territory must necessarily follow ; since devastation and rapine now universally prevail without restraint. Your subjects are trampled under foot, and every province of your empire is impoverished, depopulation spreads, and difficulties accumulate. When indigence has reached the habitation of the sovereign and his princes, what can be the condition of nobles ? As to the soldiery they are in murmur, the merchants complaining, the Muhammadan discontented, the Hindus destitute, and multitude of people, wretched even to the want of their nightly meal, are beating their heads in rage and desperation.

'How can the dignity of the sovereign be preserved, who employs his power in exacting heavy tribute from a people thus miserably reduced ? At this juncture it is told from east to west, that the emperor of Hindustan, jealous of the poor Hindu devotee will exact a tribute froms Brahmans, Sonars, Jogis, Bairagis, Sanyasis, that regardless of the illustrious honour of the Timurid race, he condescends to exercise his power over the solitary inoffensive anchorite. If your majesty places any faith in these books by distinction called divine, you will there be instructed that God is the God of all mankind, not of Muhammadans alone. The Kafir and the Muhammadan are equal in His presence. Distinction of colour are of His ordination. It is He who gives existence. In your mosques to His name the voice is raised in prayer, in a house of images, where the bell is shaken, still He is the subject of adoration. To vilify the religion or customs of other men is to set at naught the pleasure of Almighty. When we deface a picture, we naturally incur the resentment of the painter and justly has the poet said "Presume not to malign the various works of the Power divine."

'In fine the tribute you demand from the Hindus is repugnant to justice, it is equally foreign from good policy as it must impoverish the country; moreover it is an innovation and infringement of laws of Hindostan. But if zeal for your own religious faith hath induced you to determine upon this measure, the demand ought, by the rules of equity, to have been made first upon Ram Singh who is esteemed the principal among the Hindus. Then let your well wisher be called upon, with whom you will have less difficulty to encounter, but to torment ants and flies is unworthy of heroic or generous mind. It is surprising that the ministers of your government should have neglected to instruct your majesty in the rules of rectitude and honour !'

This letter was first brought to the notice of scholars by Qrme in his *Fragment of the Mughul Empire*, He attributed it to Jaswant Singh who had, however, died before the imposition of the Jizya. Tod's Munshi secured a copy of the original Persian for his master. Tod ascribed it to Raj Singh. Sir Jadunath Sankar obtained another copy in Marathi papers where it had some additional phrases which seemed to imply that it was written by one who had lately left the emperor's presence. This was supposed to refer to Shivaji. But Shivaji had no reason to protest against the imposition as 'an innovation' which was a normal charge in Bijapur to which many of the territories under him had once belonged. The scrupulous abstention from using the word Jizya for the imposition is suggestive. Further Jizya was never levied on Sanyasis, Bairagis and anchorite—the poor and the homeless beggars. Tod and Ojha ascribe the letter to Raj Singh but in view of the fact that prince Jai Singh was at Delhi when Jizya was imposed. and a war with Mewar followed soon after, it is difficult to place the letter in time. It seems to be an obvious forgery innocently practised on those keenly in search of historical documents.

The translation given above is that of Boughton Rouse made for Qrme and given by him in his note XLIX to his *Historical Fragment of the Mughal Empire*, pages 87 to 92 of the Bangabāsi edition of the work.

VIII

THE RAJPUT WAR

Raj Singh to the Defence

So far as the Rajput War is concerned Ranchhod touches upon only certain aspects of it; Bhim's exploits in Gujrat and Idar, Mughal-Mewar engagements at Raj Nagar, Debari Ghat, Chitor, Ghanera and Begun near Gogunda, Ambesi, Chirva (near Udaipur) and Deosuri. The making of peace is also described. To understand all these incidents it is necessary to supplement Ranchhod's account from other Rajput and Mughal sources.

The Scorched Earth Policy

When the Rana heard of the march of the imperial forces, he decided to adopt a scorched earth policy so far as the plains in Mewar were concerned. Despite the fact that Jai Singh was at the imperial court, in April, 1679, Khan Jahan had reported that the Rana was helping the Rathors even though Aurangzeb had warned him not to do so. The royal family were evacuated from Udaipur and it sought safety in the interior. The Rathor and Sissodia forces seem to have affected a junction near Debari pass[184] where the Rana had earlier put up a strong steel gate making the pass look as if it was an entrance to a fort. The main Mughal targets seem to have been Raj Nagar, Udaipur and Chitor. But the Debari and Deosuri passes soon got into the news and most of the major Mughal offences were concentrated upon or near them.

Aurangzeb's Plan of Campaign

Aurangzeb is said to have entered Mewar on 11 Paush (dark) 1736[185]. But Tahawar Khan and Akbar had been told off for a campaign in Mewar while the emperor was still on his way to Ajmer.[136] The Mughal commanders, Ran-

184. *Raj Vilas*, X, 66-68.

185. Ishar Das, 77 a, Rancchod, XXII, 9.

186. Cf above note 182 and 183.

chhod tells us, reached Raj Nagar[187] which they occupied. They committed many atrocities here. An engagement followed wherein the Rajput forces were led by Sakta Chundavat. In the terrific clash of arms several Rajputs were killed and Sakta was hard pressed. Ultimately he left the field free to the Mughal commander[188]. Surprisingly this engagement finds no mention in Persian records.

Engagement at Deosuri

While Aurganzeb was at Ajmer, scouts were sent to report on the whereabouts of Durga Das. They brought the news that the Rathors were occupying the Deolai pass near Deosuri[189]. Aurangzeb therefore sent prince Akbar, Tahawar Khan, Shajaat Khan, Muhtsib Khan, Muhammad Naim and Muhammad Kam Bakshi against the Rana. Akbar was specifically told off to go to Deosuri in order to prevent a junction of the Rana's forces with the Rathors. Tahawar Khan was ordered to cross Deolai and attack the Rathors beyond the pass. He reached the pass at night fall. Before proceeding forward to the village Deolai, he issued orders that not a single Rajput should be allowed to escape. The Mughals spent the night in the pass. When they reached the village they found it deserted. Some peasants were found working in the fields. On enquiry they told the Mughals that the Rana and the Rathors would be in the Deosuri pass that night but where they would go from there was not certain. The Mughals then marched immediately to Deosuri to engage the Rajputs. Qarawal Khan decided to halt at Deolai and consolidate his position there. He was afraid that if the Mughals marched against Deosuri, the Rajput force already there would fall upon his tired soldiers and take them at a disadvantage. Qarawal Khan was now sent in command of an advance party. When he came near the village, he found that the Rajput army was encamped about 3 miles from there. On learning this there was a panic in the Mughal army and many soldiers deserted in fright. Though Tahawar

187. Ranchhod, XXII, 11 and 12.
188. Ibid, XXII, 12 to 14.
189. Ishar Das, 77 A.

Khan sent a message saying that he was hastening to the rescue of the advance party, the Mughals were so panic-stricken that even Qarawal Khan left the field and sought safety in Tahawar Khan's camp. Tahawar Khan promised reinforcements and sent him back. When Qarawal Khan reached the pass a bloody engagement followed. The Rajput onslaught was so fierce that even Mughal matchlockmen fled from the field. Qarawal Khan was wounded. When Tahawar Khan came up, the battle became still more fierce. Four hundred Mughals are said to have been killed and many more Rajputs. The Rajputs now vacated the pass and left the field in order to carry on the bitter fight from elsewhere. Tahawar Khan now joined Akbar at Raj Nagar[190].

Ranchhod does not mention the engagement but refers to gathering of the Rajput forces near about the pass[191] only.

Aurangzeb's March into Mewar

News reached Aurangzeb at Ajmer that the Rana had strengthened the defences at Debari pass and was carrying out repairs to the fort of Chitor in order to strengthen it. Aurangzeb now decided to march to Udaipur on 30 November, 1679. He had called prince Mauzam from Bengal to join him at Ajmer. Mauzam joined the emperor at Pur. Aurangzeb seems to have halted here for some time. Hasan Ali Khan was now sent at the head of 7,000 horse and heavy artillery to plunder Rana's territory. From Merta, Akbar joined the emperor at Deorai[192].

From Pur, Aurangzeb advanced to Mandal. When he left it on 3 January, 1680 Muhammad Amin reported that his scouts had been up on the mountains and found that the entire country side seemed deserted. The Rana seemed to have left Udaipur. Aurangzeb reached Debari pass on 4 January. From here Hasan Quli Khan was sent to seek out the Rana and punish him. Aurangzeb himself seems to have stayed here for some time. Azam and Khan Jahan were asked

190. Ibid 77 b to 78 b.

191. Ranchhod, XXII, 15, 16.

192. Ishar Das, 78 b; *Kalimat-i-Tayabat*, 35 b; *Maasar-i-Alamgiri*, 182.

to advance upon Udaipur. After some time Ruhullah Khan and Itqad Khan (probably censors or officers of the Public Works Department) were sent with instructions to pull down the temple in front of the Rana's palace. It was one of the wonders of the age and had cost a large amount of money[193].

Mughal Vandalism at Udaipur

The Rana had already left Udaipur. The city stood deserted. Thus when the Mughal officials and masons reached the spot to destroy the temple, they were able to advance to the temple unopposed. But when the work of pulling down the temple began, a Rajput issued forth from the interior of the temple and took the Mughal workmen unawares. Several Mughals lost their lives before this single defender of the shrine could be overpowered and killed. What the Mughal considered the end of the affair proved only its beginning. As the first Rajput fell down another issued forth from the temple and worked havoc among the desecrators of his religion's shrine. Twenty members of this suicide squad sold their lives dearly before the Mughal party could proceed with the work of destroying the idols in the temple and pulling down the temple itself[194].

Meanwhile Aurangzeb advanced towards Udaipur. He found it utterly deserted. His vandalism was now exercised on the Raja's palace. The iron gates with which the Rana had strengthened the defence of the approaches to Udaipur at Deobari were also destroyed. Ranchhod refers to Aurangzeb's march to Udaipur as well as to the vandalism of the Mughal army[195]. He says that the emperor stayed at Deobari for 21 days[196].

Tahawar Khan's Plight

Hasan Ali Khan who had been sent in pursuit of the Rana had a hard time of it following the trail left by Raj Singh. He lost contact with the main Mughal army and was

193. Ishar Das, 79 a, *Maasir-i-Alamgiri* 182.
194. Ishar Das, 79 a, *Maasir-i-Alamgiri*, 185, 186.
195. Ishar Das, 79 a, Ranchhod, XXII, 17.
196. Ranchhod, XXII, 18,

not heard of for some time. Aurangzeb was very much perturbed and asked Khan-i-Jahan to go into the interior and establish contact with Hasan Ali Khan. Khan-i-Jahan not only refused to do so but had hard words with the emperor about the policy which was costing the Mughals so dear. Several other officers refused to undertake this difficult mission. Mirza Shahab-ud-Din was at last persuaded to undertake this duty on 3 January, 1680. It took him two days—according to another account 20 days—to discover the whereabouts of Hasan-Ali Khan and report back to Aurangzeb. Shahabud-Din was richly rewarded and granted an increase in salary. He was now ordered to join Hasan Ali Khan[197].

Though the plains had been all deserted, the Rajputs were not beyond taking the Mughal camps by surprise[198]. Ranchhod tells us that Kala Pratap carried away two elephants from Akbar's camp between Ambesi and Chirva and presented them to Raj Singh[199].

A pitched battle is said to have been fought at Nainwara according to Ranchhod in which 500 men died on both sides[200]. No such engagement is mentioned by other contemporary accounts.

Aurangzeb at Udaipur and Chitor

Aurangzeb was at the Udai Sagar on 24 January, 1680. After enjoying the sight, Aurangzeb fulfilled his religious obligations by ordering the destruction of three temples on its banks. On 22 February Aurangzeb left Udaipur for Chitor. Here sixtythree temples were destroyed by his orders. After thus earning religious merit Aurangzeb came back to Udaipur, tired of the fruitless pursuit of the Rana whom he could not catch up in the mountains and defiles of Mewar. Hasan Ali Khan joined the main Mughal army from Chhappana.[201] On 4 March prince Akbar with Hasan Ali Khan and Razi-ud-Khan were sent to Chitor[202]

197. Ishar Das, 79 a and b, *Maasir-i-Alamgiri*, 186. Ishar says twenty days.
198. *Maasri-i-Almgiri*, 186.
199. Ranchhod, XXII,21.
200. Ibid, XXII, 22, 23.
201. *Maasir-i-Alamgiri*, 188, 189, 190.
202. Ibid, 190.

Jai Singh's Exploit

Ranchhod speaks of another engagement fought between Kanwar Jai Singh and prince Akbar somewhere near Chitor. Jai Singh is said to have led 13,000 horse and 20,000 foot. One thousand Mughals are said to have lost their lives when Rajputs took the Mughal army by surprise one night. The Rajputs carried away three elephants and fifty horses from the Mughal army[203]. In another such ambush Gangadas Saktavat carried away eighteen Mughal elephants and several horses and camels from the imperial camp[204].

Aurangzeb back at Ajmer

Though the Rana had escaped, Aurangzeb probably felt that his main task was now over. He left Udaipur on 6 March and reached Ajmer on 12 March. His march to Ajmer might have been hastened by the news of the depredations which the Rana's son Bhim was causing in the Mughal territories.

Bhim in Idar and Gujarat

Bhim made a common cause with the dispossessed Raja of Idar and drove the imperialists out of the fort and the State. He attacked Sidhpur next. From there Bhim passed on to Badnagar where he levied a fine of Rs. 40,000 on the city. His next target was Ahmedabad itself. He realised a fine of Rs. 20,000 from the city and carried away much plunder besides. Idar and Badnagar were mostly Hindu areas. Ahmedabad had considerable Muslim population. It had at the time been capital of an independent State and was now the capital of the Mughal province of Gujarat. The large number of mosques in the city now excited Bhim's spirit of revenge for the destruction of Hindu temples in Mewar. Ranchhod tells us that he destroyed one big mosque and 200 small mosques in the city[205].

The Mughal Forces in Mewar and Marwar

Aurangzeb's retirement to Ajmer did not improve matters in Mewar. Though two princes of the blood were among

203. Ranchhod XXII, 30 to 38.
204. Ibid, XXII, 39, 40.
205. Ibid XXII, 25 to 29. *Raj Vilas*, 224-231.

the commanders in the field and the army included several veteran Mughal commanders, Aurangzeb insisted on directing the entire operations in Rajputana himself. This policy might have paid dividends when pitched battles had to be fought against the Rajputs but it failed utterly and miserably.

Sir Jadu Nath Sarkar estimated that the Mughal army engaged in the war never exceeded 15,000.[206] This is too low an estimate. For one thing if Shahjahan in 1654 had thought it fit to mobilize an army of 30,000 for an attack on Chitor, it seems unjust to Aurangzeb to hold that he was content with mobilizing only 15,000 soldiers for a struggle, which he had every reason to believe, would be grim. As the war dragged on, it should have been possible for Aurangzeb to supplement his armies so as to bring it to the necessary strength any time during the struggle. The Mughals were not committed to any military action anywhere else in India at this time. The long list of commanders mentioned in Akbar's correspondence preserved in the *Adab-i-Alamgiri*[207] does not support such a low figure. Besides prince Akbar and prince Azam, Badshah Quli Khan, Hasan Ali Khan, Ruh-ullah-Khan, Muhammad Naim, Muhammad Shuja, Murtza Quli, Muhtshim Khan and Muhammad Amin figure among the Muslim commanders in the contemporary letters. Raja Indar Singh, Rup Singh Hada, Rao Sujan Singh, Sangram Singh Kachhwala, Ram Singh, Prithvi Singh, Rathor Dip Chand and Muhkam Singh among the Hindu commanders are mentioned in the letters written from the battlefield. It is difficult to believe that these commanders had less than 15000 soldiers under them. It is possible that the troops may have been so disposed that not more than 15000 soldiers were available for action in one place at one time.

Aurangzeb in Ajmer must have kept a fairly large number of troops with him. Akbar in Sojhat and Azam in Mewar may also have kept a sufficient number of soldiers in attendance upon them particularly because there always was the danger of surprise attacks. Akbar had actually been subjected to such an attack at night at Chitor. One weakness in

206. *Aurangzeb* III, 342, 343.
207. *Adab-i-Alamgiri* (MS), 266 to 293.

Mughal plan of campaign therefore was the demand that three imperial persons be carefully guarded, happen what may to the plan of the campaign.

Aurangzeb Controls the Operations in Detail.

The Mughal emperors had frequently in the past conferred command of expeditions or government of provinces on Mughal princes. Aurangzeb had fought his way to the throne climbing up the ladder of provincial government. There may not seem to be much wrong with Aurangzeb nominating first Akbar then Azam to the command of the army in Mewar. But when Mughal princes had been earlier nominated to take command, they did not have the emperor looking over their shoulders. There is some thing pathetic in a letter of Akbar when he declares that he would ask Badshah Quli Khan to proceed to Jhilwara but if he refused, he would proceed to the place[208] himself. Still more pathetic is his lament that he intended setting up Mughal posts at Someshwar and Deosuri but did not do so because Badshah Quli Khan opposed the scheme. Rather naively he adds that though he is 25 years old, he was afraid that if his overruling of Badshah Quli Khan brought about a disaster, he would not be spared by the emperor.' He thought it necessary to secure the emperor's approval to the scheme which was refused.[209]

Rājputs Plan an Agressive Defence

A new factor in the campaign was the Rajput renunciation of an old traditon that a Rajput should fight his enemies to death preferably when the two met for the first time. However, romantic the custom of *Jauahar* may sound, it was an open admission of the fact that, once hard pressed, the Rajputs had no other alternative but to die manfully. The tradition seems to exist more in bardic literature than in actual military history. But Raj Singh and his advisors seem to have deliberately and openly renounced this tradition as soon as the war broke out. They had no

208. *Adab*, 268 a, letter No. 646, 273 a, letter No. 664.
209. *Adab*, 287 a and b, letter No. 734.

intention of seeking the joys of paradise by facing the enemy and dying in the battlefield. Like Shivaji Maratha they decided that no matter how many battles they lost, they would fight to win the war. Like the Marathas, they decided to take full advantage of the physical features of the country. Even when all seemed to have been lost in the first six months of the war, with Udaipur and Chitor in Mughal hands and the defences at Debari broken, Raj Singh was far from dismayed.

In a council of war the Rana had developed a fivefold plan of aggressive defence. The plan of war had been devised at a council in which were present prime minister, Dayaldas, Raj Purohit Gharib Das, Kanwars Jai Singh and Bhim Singh, Raval Jaswant Singh of Dungar Pur, Rana's brother, Ari Singh with his four sons, Bhagwant Singh, Subhag Singh, Gharib Singh, Guman Singh, Rao Saval Singh Chauhan, Raval Kishan Singh Chauhan of Parsoli, Ravat Sanval Das of Badnur, Chandar Sain Jhala, Ravat Kesari Singh of Solambra and his son Ganga Das, Jai Singh Jhala of Dilwara, Vairisal Parmar of Bijolia, Ravat Maha Singh, Ravat Ratan Singh Chundavat representing the house of of Solambar, Ravat Man Singh, Rao Mohkam Singh of Bhindar, Rai Durga Das Rathor, Rathor Soning Champavat, Vikramaditya Solanki, Ravat Rukman God of Kolhariya, Jhala Jaswant from Gogunda, Rathor Gopi Nath of Ghaverao, Amar Singh of Nimadi, Ram Singh, Maha Singh of Toda and Abu Malik Aziz.[210]

Surprise Rajput Attacks

To begin with, he started a scorched earth policy in the plains rendering their occupation by the Mughals entirely useless for want of supplies. He divided his armies in several contingents so that they could surprise the Mughals at several places at once. Orders were given to harass the Mughal armies by falling upon its convoys and cutting down Mughal sources of supply. Rathor and Sasodia

210. *Raj Vilas*; 188 to 225. The list of chiefs is to be found at *pages 193* to *195*. *Indentification of names follows Vir Vinod.*

forces seem to have been concentrated in fairly large numbers on the mountains guarding Deosuri pass and on the other side of the pass. The Mughals seem to have an exaggerated idea of how big these forces were.[211] But to crown it all, the Rana sent Bhim far into the Mughal territories in Gujarat on lightening raids, of which the only objective was to harass and distract the Mughals and answer Mughal method of frightfulness with equivalent terror.[212] Raj Singh did not disdain even from creating a diversion by feigning to open negotiation with Badshah Quli Khan who had to be cautioned by the emperor that he should not be taken in by such tactics.[213]

No wonder that the Rajput tactics affected the Mughal morale. When Dayal Das surprised Mughal outposts at and round about Sadri, no Mughal commander dared to go there to meet the enemy. Badshah Quli Khan and Shajaat Khan refused. Mukhtar Khan and Salabat Khan feigned illness. When at last Muhammad Shuja agreed to go there, it was only on the understanding that he would perform patrol duty in the area and not be asked to man a post at Sadri proper.[214] In a letter of 4 June 1680, Akbar complained that all Mughal commanders were afraid of engaging the Rajputs. No one was ready to move out. A usual excuse offered was the difficulties of movement. But to Akbar, it seems as if all had lost the use of their hands and feet, so useless had they become.[215]

A convoy of ten thousand kine and a train of supplies from Malwa was on its way to the Mughal army when the Rajput surprised the convoy, drove away the cows and carried off all the supplies. This at last compelled Hasan Quli Khan to move out against the enemy. This left Hasan Quli Khan's own post unprotected. Several Mughal comma-

211. *Raj Vilas*, 195 ff : *Adab*, 267 A, letter No. 640 289 a letter No. 740.

212. Cf above.

213. *Adab-i-Alamgiri*, 283 b, letter No. 716 of 30 May, 1680.

214. Ibid, 287 a and b, letter No. 734.

215. Ibid, 273 b, 274 a, letter No. 667 of 4 June, 1680; 273 a, letter No. 666, Ishar Das, 79 b.

ders refused to stir out for strengthening the Mughal posts and guarding the highway as if it was too dangerous a task for them. Akbar rightly complained that the presence of such commanders was worse than useless. Their fears and refusal to carry out instructions were *likely to prove infectious.*[21]

A very large army containing the flower of Rajput chivalry was placed under the command of Jai Singh. Ranchhod places its strength at 13,000 horse and 20,000 foot. Jhala Chander Sen, Chohan Sabal Singh, Rao Kesari Singh and Rathor Gopi Nath accompanied Jai Singh. They surprised the Mughal camp at Chitor with the result that 1000 Mughal soldiers were killed and Akbar was compelled to retire towards Ajmer.[217]

Peace Negotiations?

As mentioned earlier, negotiations for peace seem to have been opened about this time. Badshah Quli Khan reported Rana's overtures to the emperor. Ranchhod tells us that Aurangzeb was now ready to make peace at the price of surrendering three districts or 3 lacs of rupees.[218] No other contemporary authority supports him and he does not explain what happened to this proposal.

Reshuffling of Mvghal Commands

Any way, Aurangzeb was sick of it all. It has been assumed that Akbar was made a scapegoat for the Mughal failure in Mewar and transferred to Sojhat in Marwar, Azam replaced him.[219]

There was some change among Mughal commanders too. Qasim Khan and Shajaat Khan were posted at Chitor. Man Singh was stationed at Pur, Badshah Quli Khan was to go to Jodhpur with Akbar and Akbar was to make Merta his headquarters.[220] At first sight Inder Singh seems to have lost out to Mughal commanders but subsequent correspondence indicates that he was still at Jodhpur, his presence thereat

216. Cf. Ibid, 273 a, letter No. 666.
217. Ranchhod, XXII, 30 to 38.
218. *Ibid*, XXII, 45 46.
219. *Adab*, 266 b, letter No. 639 received by Akbar on 17 June, 80.
220. *Adab* 270 a, letter No. 650.

being all the more necessary in the interests of Mughal supplies. We hear of him later on as commanding in Jodhpur at Phalodi and Pohkarn.

Rathors and Sassodias were making joint efforts against the common enemy.[221] A perusal of Akbar's correspondence preserved in the *Adab-i-Alamgiri* strengthens the belief that his transfer to Jodhpur was not a sign of emperor's displeasure but of change of plans. With his moving into Jodhpur. the scene of action seems to shift into Marwar, only partly because we have his letters alone. But no contemporary or semi-contemporary records tell us anything about what this shaking up of the Mughal commands in Mewar added upto.

Bhim in Marwar

With the Mughal pressure on the Rathors increasing, the Rana's plans also embraced Marwar. When disturbances were reported at Hodal, Bhim's presence there was particularly mentioned.[222]. An engagement in the pass beyond Khod, headquarters of Badshah Quli Khan, was reported on 24 September in which the imperialists were set upon by Rajputs under Bhim. His command included Rathors as well. The pass at Deosari seems to have been the main objective of the Mughal army. Badshah Quli Khan was ordered from Khurda upto Khod to arrange for supplies. The Mughals seem to have reached near Deosari in August. Aurangzeb started urging upon Akbar and Badshah Quli Khan to enter the pass and attack the Rajputs on 20 August. But as he was controlling all the operations himself, Akbar could find excuses enough to get out of Aurangzeb's orders. We find Aurangzeb's overruling Akbar so far as stationing Mughal posts at Sadri and Someshwar were concerned. Hasan Quli Khan was sent detailed instructions about the employment and use of labourers at his post.[224] If Akbar's letter to Sambhaji is to be believed, one reason for delay might have been the

221. *Adab*, 279 a, letter No. 661 of 14 September, 1680. 267 b and 268 a, letter No. 643 of 16 July, 1680.

222. *Adab*, letter No. 740, folio 289,

223. *Adab*, 274 b, 275 a, letter No. 670, 281 a, letter No. 700.

224. *Adab*, 272 a, letter No. 661 of 14 September, 1680.

negotiation between Akbar and Raj Singh through Badshah Quli Khan for proclaiming Akbar's assumption of power.[225] On 30 October, 1680 Rana Raj Singh died and was succeeded by his son Jai Singh. This might have put an end to the negotiations.

Deosuri

Aurangzeb became keen on forcing the Deosari pass. His patience exhausted by three mɔnths of delay, he at last sent Ruh allah Khan to force both Badshah Quli Khan and Akbar to attack the pass.

On 22 November, Ruhallah Khan and Badshah Quli Khan moved on to the pass. The Mughal army consisted of 6, 000 horse and 3,000 matchlockmen. They had to face a very large Rajput army under the command of Bhim. The Rajputs were driven out and the pass was forced open, rendering the Mughal advance to Jhilwara possible. The Mughal dead were brought back by Shajaat Khan on 24 November. Akbar wrote on 30 November to Zeb-un-Nissa telling heı that the Mughal army was plundering the countryside. He boasted that not a stick would be left in any house. The entire countryside would be rendered desolate.[226]

Ranchhod tells us that Jai Singh heard of the Mughal's crossing of the Deosuri pass in November, 1680. He would have us believe that it was Tahawar Khan who crossed into the plains at the head of a Mughal army. Bhim was sent to oppose him and stop his progress. A bloody battle followed but after eight days Tahawar Khan got away.[227]

Then Jai Singh learnt that Dalair Khan was advancing at the head of another army towards Gogunda. Ravat Ratansi was sent to prevent Dalair Khan's crossing the pass. They cornered Dalair Khan. He tried to escape through a

225. *Khatut-i-Shivaji* (MS) letter 2.

226. *Adab*, 251 (a) letter No. 700; 271 b, letter 660.

227. Ranchhod XXIII, 115. A letter of 30 November. 1680 in *Adab* 231 a, mentions this engagement in which 9000 Mughals were engaged against a large body of Rajputs under Bhim. It speaks of the Mughals crossing over to Jhilwara.

little used opening at night but found Ratan Singh's men guarding this exit as well. He managed to get out anyhow and joined the emperor at Ajmer. When the emperor reprimanded him for returning emptyhanded to Ajmer, Dalair Khan explained that he could do nothing as 400 Mughals were dying daily for want of supplies.[228]

Akbar's Rebellion

Rana Raj Singh had earlier opened up negotiation for peace through Badshah Quli Khan,[229] Now when Badshah Quli Khan crossed Deosuri, contact between Jai Singh and Badshah Quli Khan seems to have been established again. Bhim Singh was in Akbar's camp on 31 December, 1680 [230] Akbar was now persuaded to proclaim himself emperor and march to Ajmer against his father on 1 January, 1681.[231] Another Mughal prince had rebelled against his father. But this proved to be the shortest of such rebellions, just as Akbar was the youngest of the Mughal princes to rebel against his father.

Aurangzeb learnt of Akbar's rebellion on 7 January, 1681 at Ajmer. He immediately strengthened his defences at Ajmer and set about calling for reinforcements from various quarters[232]. By 13 January, 1681 Aurangzeb had gathered together 16,000 soldiers under his command at Ajmer. Shah Alam was hastening to join his father from Rajasamund.[233]

When Aurangzeb reached Deosuri his scouts brought the news that Akbar was encamped at Kirki at the head of 25,000 soldiers. On 15 January Aurangzeb reached Doraha. Akbar moved up to within three miles of the emperor's camp and halted there with a view to force an engagement next morning[234].

228. Ranchhod XXIII, 16 to 31. The last verse is taken as 30th in the inscription, two verses bearing the same number.

229. Op. cit.

230. *Adab*, 276 a, letter No. 676 of 31 December, 1680.

231. *Khatut-i-Shivaji*, letter from Akbar to Sambhaji.

232. *Fatuhat-i-Alamgiri*, 181 a, *Maasir-i-Alamgiri* 200.

233. *Massir-i-Alamgiri*, 200, Ishar Das, 81 b.

234. Akbar's letter to Sambhaji in *Khatut-i-Shivaji*, Mamuri (in Khafi Khan), II, 269. Ishar Das, 82 a.

During the night, Aurangzeb's diplomacy and Akbar's foolishness combined together to make a mincemeat of the new emperor's plans. Aurangzeb wrote a letter to Akbar praising him for his clever ruse in bringing the Rajputs so near to destruction and suggested that he should manage to put them in his van the next morning so that the two Mughal armies between them could crush them easily ! As usual this letter was allowed to fall into the hands of Durga Das. He was naturally upset and hastened to Akbar's camp to confront him. The guards refused to awaken the new emperor at this late hour. Durga Das then went to Tahawar Khan's camp only to learn there that he was missing. Desertion of Mughal officers had been going on as Akbar had been approaching the imperial army. Durga Das's fears were now confirmed. The Rajputs struck camp and deserted Akbar to his fate. This was followed by more desertions, so when Akbar woke up next morning he was left with only a small body of his personal followers[235]. No longer an emperor, he became a fugitive to escape his emperor's wrath.

Akbar's Flight to Deccan

Durga Das discovered Aurangzeb's ruse next day and joined Akbar again. By devious paths Akbar reached Jai Singh's camp who, Akbar told Sambhaji later on, offered to keep Akbar as an honoured guest. Not feeling safe there Akbar fled to the Deccan[236].

Aurangzeb was well rid of Akbar. He punished his followers and tried to capture Akbar. An agent of the Jaipur ruler reported from the court that when Aurangzeb learnt that Akbar had reached the Deccan unscathed, his anger knew no bounds. It appeared as if he had lost his senses. He put his beard in his mouth and started nibbling at it[237]. Ranchhod exhibits no knowledge of Akbar's rebel-

235. Ishar Das, 82 b to 83 b.

236. Akbar's letters to Sambhaji in *Khatut-i-Shivaji*. Rajput accounts do not support Akbar's assertion that the Rana offered to keep him at his court. Ishar Das, 85 b, 86a, 109 b, 110 a. *Maasir-i-Alamgiri*, 202 to 207.

237. *Jaipur Records*, III, 108.

lion. At one place he starts talking of negotiations for peace between Akbar and Jai Singh[238] but soon corrects himself by describing the peace.[239] As a chronicler of Mewar he does not seem to have been interested in what proved to be the turning point in the war between Mewar and Delhi.

Maharana Jai Singh

Aurangzeb, it seems, now had had enough of this protracted war against the Rathors and Sasodias both. Mughal accounts have it that it was Durga Das only who accompanied Akbar in his march against Aurangzeb. The new Rana gave no signs of sitting in peace and letting Mughals have their way. His commanders continued harassing the enemy, now alone, now in combination with the Rathors who were still up in arms. Whatever the Rana's intentions might have been,[240] Aurangzeb now decided to overlook them in order to purchase peace at least with the Rana.

Negotiation For Peace

Negotiations were now opened through Shyam Singh,[241] a Sasodia dignitary in the Mughal army and a grandson of Rana Karn. Shyam Singh was thus the Rana's uncle. He is said to have informed the Rana that, though the emperor

238. Ranchhod, XXIII, 32 wrongly (numbered 31 in the inscription) It has been suggested that the verse refers to Akbar's attempt at roping the Rana in the attempt to rise against his father. *Mewar and the Mughal Emperors* seems to imply that. But the reason for this move given by Ranchhod is that 400 Mughals were dying daily and therefore on behalf of a distraught emperor Akbar wanted to make peace. This cannot therefore turn Mewar-Akbar negotiations into Raj Singh's instigation to Akbar to rebel against his father.

239. Ranchhod, XXIII, 44 (wrongly numbered 43) 51 and 66.

240. *Maasir-i-Alamgiri* 205 records an engagement between Dewan Dayal Das and the imperialist after Akbar fiasco in January. Ishar Das 85 b, 86 c, records similar engagement at Merta in Marwar between Ajab Singh, Muhkam Singh Mertia and the imperialists in which the Rajputs were worsted. But Ishar Das places the first engagement before the death of Raj Singh and of the two he is more trustworthy. Ojha follows Sarkar and Devi Prasad and wrongly places it in Jai Singh's reign *Masir-i-Alamgiri* records the news received on 19 January, 1681 of an engagement at Mandal where the Thander was reported dead, 238.

241. Sarkar (III, 370) wrongly describes him as the ruler of Bikaner. He would have been an odd choice for such negotiations.

was anxious to end the war, he would not himself take the initiative. At Shyam Singh's suggestion the Rana sent Rao Kesari Singh, Hukam Singh and Ghasi Ram with a letter to the emperor. This seems to have been presented at court through Azam.

By order of the emperor, a letter to the Rana was written by Azam on 5 March, 1681 assuring him that the emperor would grant him all the favours to which Rana Amar Singh had been entitled as soon as the Rana would present himself at (Azam's) court.[242] On this the Rana sent another delegation consisting of Gopi Nath, Sanval Das Pancholi, Chandar Sain Jhala, Jait Jhala, Sambal Das Rathor, Ravat Kesari Singh and Kesari Singh Chohan. This brought forth a note from Dalair Khan asking the Rana to hasten to meet the prince at Rajasamund within four days.[243]

Jai Singh calls upon Azam.

Now occurred a snag. Jai Singh declared that though he had no such fears, his foolish Rajputs would not let him present himself at the prince's camp unless there was a guarantee of good faith.[244] Dalai Khan surrendered two of his sons to the Rajputs, whereupon, leaving them well guarded, the Rana left his place of safety at Ghati on 13 June for meeting the prince.[245] It is necessary to note that at the back of it all was Aurangzeb's firm determination to put an end to the Mughal-Mewar feud. An agent of the Jaipur state wrote to his master that Aurangzeb had instructed Azam to conclude peace with the Rana on whatever terms were agreeable to the Rana if he consented to meet Azam.[246] Not content with this Aurangzeb instructed Azam as to how

242. Letter in Mewar Archives, reproduced in *Vir Vinod,* II, 651, 652. This letter refers to Rana's representation. Ojha wrongly refers to it as a Farman (royal order written on behalf of the emperor).

243. Letters in Mewar Archives, reproduced in Vir Vinod II, 654, 655.

244. *Vir Vinod,* II, 655.

245. *Maasir-i-Alamgiri* 207.

246. *Jaipur Records,* III, 109, 110.

247. *Maasir-i-Alamgiri* 240.

to receive the Rana. Azam was told to embrace the Rana and seat him on his right.

The Rana met Azam on 14 June at Rajsamund. *Massir-i-Alamgiri* declares that the Rana surrendered the districts of Mandal, Pur and Badnor. He was recognised as a commander of 5000 horse as most of his predecessors had been.[247] The contemporary correspondence reproduced in the *Vir Vinod*[248] seems to indicate that Aurangzeb had formally assessed an indemnity of 3 crore dams against Jai Singh. Of this 40 lacs dams were excused and 2,60,00,000 dams had to be paid. Against this Mubarakpur, Mandal and Badnor were granted to him. But we find Badnor given to another Sasodia chief, Daulat Singh on 17 August, 1681.[249] It is therefore difficult to accept the statement that the Rana was ever allowed to take possession of this or of any other of these three parganas.

Approval of Terms of Peace.

But Mughal protocol did not end the matters here. On 13 July, 1681 a letter of Jai Singh[250] addressed to the emperor was entrusted to Khidmat Khan for proper action. On 15 July, Jai Singh's Peshkash was presented at the court and orders were passed that all Mughal officers stationed in his territories be recalled.[251] On 3 August, 1681 it was reported that Rana Jai Singh had given 1 lac of ashrafis as a Peshkash in lieu of Jizya.[252] This was said to be less than the assessed dues by Rs. 3,000. The emperor remitted the difference.

Formal Restoration of Peace.

It seems Azam sent the amount on to the emperor

247. *Maasir-i-Alamgiri*, 207.
248. *Vir Vinod*, II, 656 to 663, 671, 672.
249. *Court Bulletin* of the same date.
250. *Court Bulletin* of the same date.
251. Ibid.
252. Ibid. Ishar Das, 79 b, suggests the amount as in the text alone.

and it was presented at the court on 6 August, 1681[253] Both sides were trying to save their faces. The indemnity mentioned in Mewar records turns up as a payment of the Jizya due from Mewar in Mughal chronicles. The term Peshkash has never been used for the payment of any tax in Mughal records. It usually refers to payment made before entering upon a Mughal office of profit. Theoretically the Rana of Mewar had lost his office of the command of 6,000 horse which Rana Raj Singh had held ever since Aurangzeb's accession to the throne. Rana Raj Singh's death put an end to this grant. A new royal order conferring on Jai Singh Udaipur as a watanjagir and creating him a 5000er with the command of 5000 horse was being issued and a Peshkash was certainly due for that. It was neither indemnity nor Jizya.

On 13 August it was reported that Jai Singh received the royal firman issued in his favour with due honours, 3 miles outside Udaipur.[254] The notes of the negotiations preserved in the Mewar records suggest that Aurangzeb gave up his claim to levy Jizya in Mewar. He may have squared his conscience by letting it be understood that the decrease in the command of the Rana of 1000 and by 1000 horse and consequent shrinkage in his holdings were equivalent

253. *Court Bulletin* of the same date.

254. *Court Bulletin* of the same date.

Tod reproduced a representation of the Rana as follows :—

Jawal-sowal of Sur Singh and Narhar Bhan with the emperor.

1. Your servants according to your royal pleasure and summons have been sent by the Rana to represent what is written underneath. We hope you will agree to these requests besides other which would be made by Padma Singh.

Let Chitor with the districts adjacent and pertaining thereto when it was inhabited, be restored.

2. In such temples and places of Hindu religious resort as have been converted into mosques, the past cannot be recalled, but let this practice be abolished.
3. The aid hitherto offered to empire by the Rana shall be continued, but let no additional demands be made.
4. The son and descendants of the deceased Raja Jaswant Singh, as soon as able to perform their duties, we hope, will have the country restored to them.

Mumzoori (written in emperor's hand) and the impress of the emperor's hand.

Tod declared that the original was in Mewar archives.

to the payment of the Jizya by him. Such an arrangement suited both sides. The Rana would not have tolerated the levying of Jizya and its collection in Mewar by Mughal officials. Such an undertaking would have provided a perpetual pin-prick in Mewar. It must be remembered that the usual mansab of Ranas of Udaipur was a command of 5000. Rana Amar Singh, Rana Jagat Singh and Rana Raj Singh, before the war of succession, had only held this mansab. All that now happened was that the additions granted to Raj Singh for his neutrality, during Aurangzeb's bid for the throne, did not pass on to his successor. The loss of the additional districts was soon made up by Bhim's becoming a commander of 4000 in Aurangzeb's service.

The agent of the Jaipur State at the imperial court reported to his master that the peace being concluded with the Rana, he was asked to send his contingent against the Rathors. The Rana asked to be excused and no more was heard about it.[255] The Mughals were very anxious to rope in Bhim Singh in their service and the Rana was asked to help them therein. Jai Singh declared that Bhim Singh had quarrelled with him and he knew nothing about his whereabouts.[256]

Ranchhod has a very interesting account of the meeting between the Rana and the prince.[257] Jai Singh is said to have been accompanied by 10,000 horse and 7,000 foot. As the Rana was meeting Azam on the banks of the Rajasamund in Mewar, such a large number of soldiers could have moved with the Rana, though not to the meeting place. It is not likely however that the Rana had kept such a large number of soldiers with him in his retreat. Dalair Khan had given the Rana only 4 days' notice for the meeting and it is not likely that during those 4 days large movement of troops would have been permitted. The local tradition has it that the Rana was afraid of Aurangzeb's tricking him at the meeting.[258] It is unlikely that any such

255. Ibid, Jaipur Records, III, 87.
256. Ibid, Bhim, however, later on joined Aurangzeb in the Deccan and rose to be a great commander. Cf. the *Founder of Banera Raj* in appendix IV.
257. Ranchhod, 35, 36 (wrongly numbered in the inscription as 34, 35).
258. *Vir Vinod*, II, 667, 668, 669.

thought would have crossed the Rana's mind if he was to have been accompanied by such a large force. The Mughal protocol did not allow of such a practice and it is not likely that Azam would have gone out of his way to thus pander to Rana's whims.

Mewar was now at peace with the Mughal emperor. Apparently Ajit Singh had been let down by the Rana. But peace with Mewar made it possible for Aurangzeb to leave northern India for the south. Consequently the pressure on Mewar was also eased. However anxious Aurangzeb's officers may have been to put down disturbances in Mewar, their zeal could not compensate for Aurangzeb's absence in the south.

Peace at last.

Mewar was left to lick its wounds. The war had lasted for more than a year. It was the longest continuous war in the history of Mewar. The damage it had done to the resources of the State was considerable. Jai Singh was however soon able to put his house in order so much so that in 1691 he was in a position to add another and a bigger artificial lake, Jai Samud, to Mewar.[259]

259. *Raj Vilas*, X, 66-68.

APPENDIX I

Abstract of some letters of Akbar from the battlefield

(A) Akbar's Plan of the Campaign.

To Sheikh Makhdum,

I wrote to Badshah Quli an urgent letter asking him to move up to the pass and set up camp near it. He is to inform me of his intention to advance into the pass a day earlier so that I can join him. I have sent Salabat Khan to reinforce him. If he is able to set up his camp early, I would join him there. I shall leave Muhtisham Khan at the pass so that he sets up thanas at Someshwar to the left of the pass and at Sadri to the right. He is then to proceed to Nadol. But if Salabat Khan declines to move, I intend stationing Muhtisham Khan at Deosuri and Sujan Singh at Nadol and with Shajaat Khan, Badshah Quli Khan and Raja Inder Singh I would reach Jhilwara beyond the pass. I would then send Badshah Quli Khan to Kumbhalmer.

Rajputs are stirring up trouble at Sadri. I have sent a force there. I asked Badshah Quli Khan to proceed thereto. On his refusal, I asked Shajaat Khan. He also refused to move against them. Muhtisham Khan and Salabat Khan feigned illness. I was at last able to put Muhammad Shuja at the head of this force. My intention was not to set up our own thana there but to influence Rajput activities in the neighbourhood by our own activity and movement.

I want to set up thanas at Deosuri and Someshwar. But Badshah Quli Khan opposed my plan. I thought that if the plan did not work, I would be blamed. (Instead of insisting that my orders be carried out) I wrote for orders to the emperor. I am twenty five years old no doubt but I need imperial orders (to carry out this plan against Badshah Quli Khan).

Adab, letter No. 734 ; ff 287 a and b (The permission to set up the thanas was refused)

(B.) The progress of the war.

(i) Letter dated 4 June, 1680.

To the emperor,

I have earlier informed you about Hasan Quli Khan's going in persuit of the Rajput forces that had surprised our supplies. He left Mandsor for the purpose. I cannot say when he would be back.

I hear that the Rana is staying at his own place but has put his son at the head of a large mobile force so that he should carry out plundering expedition against us and also keep watch on our movements.

On our side, every commander is afraid of an engagement against the enemy and trots out the difficulties of movement against the enemy's position as his excuse. I fail to understand what has overtaken them. All seem to have lost the power of "moving their hands and feet". Even when orders are definite, specific and urgent, they find out excuses.

If you permit me, I should like to send my mother and other relatives (for safety) to Ajmer, leave a small force at Chitor and myself move against the Rajputs in order to subdue them.

(*Adab*, letter No. 667, ff 273b and 274 a).

(ii) To the emperor,

I wrote to Hasan Quli Khan several times that he should enter the pass and turn out the enemy forces from the area beyond. He refuses to move and prefers to remain inactive where he is. He pleads difficulties of movement to the approaches to the pass and the still more those of advancing in the mountains and the pass itself. On account of his sitting still things have come to this pass that the supply convoy with grain and ten thousand heads of cattle from Malwa was set upon by the Rajputs in a surprise attack. They succeeded in carrying away all the supplies and the cattle. Hasan Quli now felt affronted and ashamed and went in persuit of the enemy (I sent Qasam Khan at the head of a force of 1000 for the protection of Hasan Quli Khan's camps in his absence).

I thought it necessary that disciplined and experienced soldiers be stationed at Nimach and other stations so that if the Rajputs stir up trouble in the neighbourhood, they should be immediately suppressed and the supply road be thus kept open. I asked Mukhtar Khan to go and strengthen these camps. He refused to move out. Such commanders are of no use; rather the contrary, they spread their contagion to others as well.

I then asked Shajaat Khan to proceed thereto but he also refused to leave his own camp. I had then to cancel my order to Kasam Khan who had been designed for the protection of Hasam Quli Khan's thanas and sent him with an additional 500 soldiers towards Nimach.
(*Adab* letter No. 666, 273 a)

(C) AKBAR'S TRANSFER TO JODHPUR.

Akbar to Shah Alam,

When after leaving Lahore, I reached the imperial presence, the emperor was ready for his campaign against the Rajputs. On the move, the emperor kept himself busy and had not a moment's rest. He personally supervised all arrangements. (On his reaching Ajmer) I was sent to Merta. From there (after some time), I joined the emperor and left for Udaipur on 16 June, 1680. From there I moved to Chitor and stayed there for some time. Aurangzeb then heard that Rathors were creating serious disturbances (in Jodhpur) and the army there was proving no match for them. I was, therefore, ordered to proceed to Marwar. I reached Sojhat and am writing this from there. There is trouble created by the Rana at Nadol on his borders and the Rathors are also creating disturbances there. I hope to move out thereto in a day or two. (He reached there on 30 September, 1680.) *Adab*, letters No. 686, 699, 700; 278 a, 280 b, 281 (a).

(D) Akbar's account of Battle of Deosuri.

(1) Letter No 700, Akbar to Zaibunnasa; 281 (a)

We attacked the Deosuri pass. We had 6000 horse and 3000 matchlockmen. We went up the mountains and blocked all means of getting out. The Rajputs under Bhim opposed us with a large army. We advanced to Jhilwara.

There were some casualities among the Muslims as well. We are busy plundering the entire countryside and do not intend to spare a single house. Everything would be laid waste and desolate. Badshah Quli Khan would move on to Kumbhalmer.

(ii) Letter No. 703, Akbar to Zaibunnasa, f. 282 (a).

Of the male and female prisoners made here, 1/8 would be distributed among the soldiers and officers. The rest would be made slaves. If there are any good enough for the purpose, I shall present them to you and other Begums.

(iii) Letter No. 726, Akbar to Sheikh Makhdum, f. 286 a.

None of the slaves was worth being presented to those at Delhi. They have all been sold (or ransomed ?)

(E) Aurangzeb's detailed guidance and control of the war.

(i) Akbar to Aurangzeb.

In accordance with your orders of 25 May, 1680, necessary arrangements have been made and a report is sent herewith.

Adab, Letter No. 636, f 266 a.

(ii). Detailed orders in a royal command acknowledged, explanation offered for departure from earlier instructions. Orders asked for new movements. Letter No. 638, *Adab*, f 266b Akbar to Aurangzeb.

(iii). Akbar ordered to Merta via the prescribed route. Supporting commander named. (Aurangzeb's letter received on 17 June, 1680) *Adab*, 266 (b), Letter No. 639, Akbar to Aurangzeb.

(iv). Badshah Quli Khan ordered to Jodhpur. Akbar asks for permission to visit Ajmer. (Aurangzeb's order of 1 June, 1680) Adab, 269 (b), Letter No. 651, Akbar to Aurangzeb.

(v). Letter No. 653, Akbar to Aurangzeb. *Adab*, f 270 (a).

Movement of commanders ordered on 17 June, 1680 Shujaat Khan and Qasim Khan to Chitor; Man Singh and; Badshah Quli Khan to Jodhpur; Akbar to Merta.

(vi). Letter No. 655, Akbar to Aurangzeb,
Adab, f. 270 (b).

Explanation offered for failure to carry out orders.

(vii). Letter No. 718, Akbar to Asadullah Khan, 6 June, 1680, appointment of Man Singh as Fojdar of Badhnor as ordered by the emperor carried out.

(viii). Letter No. 641 to Aurangzeb, ff, 267 (a) and (b). Reports carrying out of imperial orders.

(ix). Letter No. 649 to Aurangzeb, ff. 268 (b) and 269 (a) acknowledges the detailed instructions given in the imperial order of 31 August, 1680.

(x). Letter No. 658 to Aurangzeb, f 271 (a), received on 25 August, 1680.

I shall go to Nadol as ordered.

(xi). Letters No. 657 (f.271 (a) ; 660 (f.270(b), f.271 a; 660. f, 270, b ; 674, f, 275 b and 675, 275 b refer to reshuffling of commanders or armies and station commanders.

(F). Akbar's apologia for moving to Ajmer in December 1680.

The emperor had written to me that now that the supplies have been received, I should not remain at Deosuri. 'But' declares Akbar, 'Badshah Quli Khan, a son and a brother of the Rana have come to me and do what I would, Rana's brother and son are not prepared to come to the imperial presence by themselves. They insist that I should accompany them to your presence. Necessary orders may therefore be issued. When the Rathors learnt that the Rana's representatives are with me on their way to submission to you, the Rathors have also come to my camp.' (*Adab*. Letter No. 676 received on 31 December, 1680, f. 276(a).

APPENDIX II

Fxtracts from *Rājapraśasti*

Shah Jahan's attack on Chitor.

(Canto VI, verses 11-26)

शते सप्तदशे पूर्णे वर्षे एकादशे त्विषे ।
अजमेरे साहिजहाँदिल्लीशं तं समागतम् । ११ ।

श्रुत्वाथ राजसिंहेन्द्रश्चित्रकूटे समागतम् ।
तं सादुल्लहखानाख्यं दिल्लीश्वरमन्त्रिणम् । १२ ।

प्रेषयामास तत्पार्श्वे भट्टं तु मधुसूदनम् ।
काठोड़ीवंशतेलंगः स गतः खानसन्निधौ । १३ ।

खानः पंडितसंबुद्ध्या भट्टं प्रत्युक्तवान् कथम् ।
गरीबदासो राणेन कथमाकारितस्तथा । १४ ।

झालाख्यरायसिंहश्च भट्टेनोक्तं तदादितः ।
जातमेवं प्रतापाख्यरानाम्नाता रणोत्कटः । १५ ।

शक्तसिंहो मेघनामा रावतो मेदपाटतः ।
आयातौ स्थापितौ दिल्लीनाथेन किल तौ पुनः । १६ ।

मेदपाटे समायातौ चकार परमेश्वरः ।
इति स्वामिप्रयुक्तानां राजन्यानां स्थलद्वयम् । १७ ।

खानेनोक्तं सत्यमेतत्पुनः खानस्ततोऽवदत् ।
राणेशस्याश्ववाराणां संख्यां कथय पण्डित । १८ ।

सद्विशतिसहस्राणि भट्टेनोक्तं स उक्तवान् ।
दिल्लीशस्याश्ववाराणां लक्षसंख्यास्ति तत्कथम् । १९ ।

कार्यं स (मा नं) भट्टेन प्रोक्तं खान शृणु स्फुटम् ।
दिल्लीशस्याश्ववाराणां लक्षं राणामहीपतेः । २० ।

सद्विशतिसहस्राणि साम्यं सृष्टिकृता कृतम् ।
खानोन्तःकोपवान् खानो जयसिंहस्तवोक्तवान् । २१ ।
खानसंगे साहिजहांदर्शनं चेत्करोत्यहो ।

राजकुमारस्तु तदा चतुर्वंश मिता मया। २२।

देशा दिल्लीश्वराद्वाप्या विद्धि रे मधुसूदन।
राणासेवां व्यधादेवं स्वामिधर्मो महान् कृतः। २३।

दिल्लीश्वरकुमारस्य संगेऽस्मत्पूर्वजन्मनाम्।
कुमारामेलनं चक्रू राजसिंहो विचार्य तत्। २४।

सुल्तानसिंहनामकमहाकुमारं तु ट्ठकुरैः सहितम्।
साहिजहांसुतदारासकोहसंगेऽथ संप्रेष्य। २५।

एवं साहिजहानेन मिलनं कृतवान्नृपः।
राजसिंहो भाग्यदानविक्रमैर्विक्रमार्कवत्। २६।

2. Marriage of Bhav Singh Baghela and the raising of the status of the Baghelas

(Canto VIII, verses, 37-43)

शते सप्तदशे पूर्णे एकविंशतिनामके।
वर्षे मार्गेऽसिताष्टम्यां राजसिंहा (हो) महीपति (:)। ३७।

अनूपसिंहभूपस्य वा(बा)घेलाबान्धवप्रभोः।
भावसिंहकुमाराय कन्यामजवकूंवरिं। ३८।

संकल्प्य विधिना दत्वा(त्वा) महाराजन्यपंक्तये।
गोत्रराजान्यकन्यानामष्टाग्रां नवतिं ददौ। ३९।

अथायं पां(पा)कशालायां राजसिंहो नरें(रे)श्वरः।
भावसिंहकुमाराद्यैर्बान्धवीयैस्तु वा(बा)हुजैः। ४०।

अस्पर्शभोजिभिः साकमुपविष्टो विशिष्टभाः।
कुर्वाणो भोजनं भाति बान्धवीयैस्तवेरित(तम्)। ४१।

श्रीराणाराजसिंहस्य यदन्नमतिपावनम्।
तज्जगन्नाथरायस्य प्रसादान्नं न स(सं)शयः। ४२।

तदन्नभोजिन्ये (नो) ऽवश्यं वय(यं) प्राप्ताः पवित्रताम्।
हय (या) न्गजान्म(न्भू)षणानि वरेभ्योऽदात्म(न्म) हीपतिः। ४३।

3. Jai Singh's Mission to Delhi.

(Canto XXII, verses 1-6)

स(श)ते सप्तदशेऽतीते प(पं)चत्रिंशन्मितेब्दके ।
शुक्लैकादशिकायां तु चैत्ते (त्रे) प्रस्थानमातनोत् । १ ।

श्रीराजसिंहस्याज्ञातो जयसिंहो(हा) भिधो (बली) ।
मा(म)हाराजकुमारोऽयं (य)मजमेरौ समागतः । २ ।

औरंगजेशं द्रष्टुं स दिल्लीं दिल्लीपतिं ययौ ।
पश्चाजे(ज्ज)यकुमारोऽयं ययौ सेनासमावृतः । ३ ।

दिल्लीतः क्रोशयुग्मस्थे(?)अत्र शिविरोत्तमे ।
दिल्लीश्वरं ददर्शायं सोस्यादरमथाकरोत् । ४ ।

मुक्तामाला उरोभूषा अस्मै हैमाव(म्ब) राण्यदात् ।
महागजेन्द्रभूषाक्तं तादृ(क्)तूं (तुं)गतुरंगमान(न्) । ५ ।

झालाख्यचन्द्रसेनाय पुरोहितवराय च ।
गरीबदाससन्नाम्ने हेमवासांसि वा हयान् । ६ ।

4. War in Mewar.

(Canto XXII, verses 10-25)

शते सप्तदशेऽतीते वर्षे षट्त्रिंशदाह्वये
पौ(ष) स्य कृष्णैकादश्यां मेवाडे दिल्लिकापतिः । १० ।

आयातस्तस्य पुत्रस्त(स्तु)आदौ अकबराभिधः ।
तथा तहवरः खानः प्राप्तः सेनासमावृतः । ११ ।

सुंदरे रा(ज)नगरे राजमंदिरमंहवः (?) ।
तल्लोकैः कल्पितास्तत्र शक्तः(क्तः) शक्तावतोत्तमः । १२ ।

पुत्रः सबलसिंहस्य पूरवतस्य सः (?)।
भ्रा(ता) मुहकमसिंहस्य घोरं रणमिहाकरोत् । १३ ।

वीरश्चोंडावतः कोपि तस्य विंशतिसद्भटाः ।
कृत्वा युद्धं दिवं याता भित्वा(त्वा)भास्व(स्क)र मंडलम् । १४ ।

विषे: कलेव(बं)लावाज्ञां ददौ राणापुर(रं) दरः ।

दहवा(री)महाघट्ट(ा)दन्यघटाच्च वा(बा)हुजाः । १५ ।
आयांतु कृतसंकल्पा अपि या(यो)द्धुं मदु(वित) तः ।
नलिकागोलकस्त्रो(स्तो)माः शूरसंघा महोन्नताः ।१६ ।

राणो(क्त)तस्तथा जातं ततो दिल्लीश आगतः ।
दहवारी महाघट्टे क्र(कृ)त्वा तद्द्वारपातन (नम्) । १७ ।

ऐ(ए)कविंशतितिथ्यन्तं स्थितोऽत्र निशि चैकदा ।
विष्योः (ष्यो) दयपुरं प्र(प्रा)प्तो गुप्त एषास्त्युपश्रुतिः । १८ ।

तदा अकबरः प्राप्तो महोदयपुरे ततः ।
तथा तहब(व्व)रः खं(खा) नस्ततत्कृत्यं तद्भटैः कृतम् । १९ ।

ऐ(ए)कलिंगं द्रष्टुमगाद्दैवादकबरस्ततः ।
अंबेरीचीरवाघट्टीर्वृ ष्ट्वा शिविरमागतः । २० ।

झालाप्रतापः कंकेटपुरवासी गजद्वयम् ।
दिल्लीशसे(सै) न्यादानीय राणो (णे)द्राय न्यव(वे)दयत् ।२१।

भवेसरस्था वल्लाख्या हयौघान्हस्तिनां (व्रजम्)
न्यं(न्य)वेदयन्न(न्नु)ष्ट्रवू (वृ)ते(वं)नैनवारास्थितप्रभोः । २२ ।

पंचाशत्कसहस्राणि (नृणा) (णां) नष्टानि तद्विषः ।
दिल्लीस्व(श्व)रस्ततः प्र(प्रा)प्तः चित्रकूटेऽन्यथा प्रथाम् । २३ ।

ज्ञापयित्वा अकबरस्था(स्तथा) तत्र समागतः ।
तथा हसन्नलीखां च छप्पन्नादत्र चागतः । २४ ।

नाही(हीं) तदायातो (?) राणो रोषपोषितः ।
कोटडीग्रामतः शीघ्रं ततः सेनासमो(मा)वृतः । २५ ।

5. Bhima in Gujarat.

(Canto XXII, verses 26-29)

संप्रेषितो भीमसिंहकुमारो राणभूभुजा ।
ईडाद्वं (ध्वं) समतनोत्सैदहसा(खां)लयो गतः । २६ ।

वडनगरं लूटितमथ चत्वारि(रिं) शत्सहस्त(स्र) मिताः ।
राजतमुद्रा जगृहे दंडविधौ भीमसिंह इह । २७ ।
अहमदनगरे लक्षद्वयप्रमितमुद्रकाणां वस्तूनाम् ।

वस्तूनां लूटनमिहे(ह) कारितवान्भीमसिंहा ह व ब ली ।२८।
एका महामसीदी विखंडिता लघु(घु) मसीदिसुत्रिशती
दे(वा)लयपातसुवः रुषः प्रकाशित(ता) भीमसिंहवीरेण । २९ ।

6. Jai Singh's Exploits.
(Canto XXII, verses 30-38)

राणामहीमहेन्द्रस्य आज्ञया विज्ञ उत्सुकः ।
महाराजकुमारश्रीजयसिंहनामः (मा) (?)। ३० ।

झालाह्यचन्द्रसेनेन चोहानेन चमूभृता ।
तथा सव(व) लसिंहेन राणेण रणसूरिणा । ३१ ।

केसरीसिंहनाम्ना तद्भ्रात्रा रावेण शोभितः ।
राठोडगोपीनाथेन अरिसिंहस्य सूनुना । ३२ ।

भगवंतादिसिंहेन धन्यराजन्यवारिभिः ।
सहितं स्वाहितजयं कर्तं (र्तुं) हितसमीहिते । ३३ ।

त्रयोदशसहस्राणि अश्ववारखरावलेः ।
सद्विंशतिसहस्राणि पदातीनां महात्मनाम् । ३४ ।

संगे गृहीत्वा प्रययौ चित्रकूटतटीं प्रति ।
ततस्ते ठक्कुरा रात्रौ संगरं चक्रुरुन्मदाः । ३५ ।

सहस्रसंख्यान्दिल्लीशः लोकान् जघ्नुर्गजत्रयम् ।
येनागतास्तांस्तुरगान् तान् सृतस्तदकब्वरः । ३६ ।

पंचाशत्तुरगान्वीरा गृहीत्वा तान्यवेदयन् ।
कुमारजयसिंहाय जयसिंहो मुदं दधे । ३७ ।
जयसिंहकुमारोथ श्रीराणेंद्रस्य दर्शनम् ।
कृतवाक्र (न्कृ) तकृत्या (त्यो) वा सहरणकृतौ कृती । ३८ ।

7. The Battle of Ghanera.
(Canto XXII, verses 39-44)

शक्तावतस्य शक्तस्य केसरीसिंहवर्मणः ।
गंगकूवरपुत्रो यः कुमारपदवीं वधत् । ३९ ।

अष्टादशद्विपान्मत्तान्हयौघानुष्ट्रसंचयान् ।
दिल्लीशसैन्यादानीय राणेन्द्राय न्यवेदयत् । ४० ।

राणेंद्रेण कुमारोऽथ भीमसिंहो बलान्वितः ।
प्रेषितोऽकबराख्येन तथा तहवरेण च । ४१ ।

खानेन संगरं चक्रे शक्ररक्षोरणोप(मं) ।
उल्लंघ्य देवसूरीं ता(तां) महानालिं नलोप्र(प) मः । ४२ ।

घानोरानगरे चक्रे युद्धं स योद्धृविक्रमः ।
वा(वी)कासोलंकिवीरोथ घट्टे रक्षां रणं व्यधात् । ४३ ।

राणेन्द्रेण कुमारोऽथ गजसि (सिं) हो व (ब) लान्वितः ।
प्रस्थापितो व(ब) भंजायं तद्वे(द्बे)गमपुरं महत् । ४४ ।

8. Aurangzeb's Overtures.
(Canto XXII, verses 45-46)

राष्ट्रत्रय (यं) रूप्यमुद्रालक्षत्रयमथापि वा ।
दत्वं(त्वं) व मिलनं कार्यं मया राणेन निश्चितम् । ४५ ।

औरंगजेबो दिल्लीश उक्तवान्स (त) द्रू(द्रु)त्तरम् ।
विषेः कलेर्बलाज्जातं यत्तदत्र वदाम्यहम् । ४६ ।

9. Jai Singh's Accession.
Canto XXIII, verses 9-10

तनः (तः) कडंजे नगरे शिविरं व्यातनोद्ब ली ।
जयसिंहो जयमयः स पञ्चदश वासरान् । ९ ।

उल्लंघं कृतवान्वीरो राजसिंहासनास्थितिम् ।
रि(र)रक्ष रणदक्षोऽयं क्षोणीमक्षौहिणीपतिः । १० ।

10. Jai Singh's Engagement Against the Mughals.
(Canto XXIII, verses 11-28)

शते सप्तदशे पूर्णे सप्तत्रिंशन्मितेब्दके ।
मार्गशा(शी)र्षे शौर्यं मार्गप्रकाशी मार्गणार्थदः । ११ ।

वसत्क(न्क) डुंजे नगरे जयसिंहो महामनाः ।
श्रुत्वा तहवरं खानं देवसूरीं विलंघ्य च । १२ ।
आयांत(तं) घट्टमर्यादालोपिनं कोपपूरितम् ।
स्वभ्रातरं भीमसिंहं भीमं वा प्रेंषयत्स तु । १३ ।
वीकासोलंकिनं दृष्ट्वा तं समाश्वास्य तत्परम् ।
महाभीमो भीमसिंहो वीकासोलंकिनीवरः । १४ ।
जघ्नतुर्म्लेंच्छसक्ता(सैन्या)नि रुद्धस्तहवरोऽभवत् ।
विनाष्टकाना मु(क्तो)थ राहुमुक्तेन्दुवच्छशी ।१५।
धानोरायश्च आयातो जयसिंहो दलेलखां ।
छपन्नदेश शैलेष्वायातो ह्यागवृतोस्य तु ? ।१६।

मार्गो दत्तो राणलोकैर्गोगुंदाघट्ट आगतः ।
रुद्धो घट्टस्ततो राणालोकैः (लो)केषु विश्रुतैः । १७ ।
रत्नसीरावतेनापि स्थितं घटे(ट्टे) शिलोत्कटे ।
दलेलखां न शक्तोभूत्तदा गन्तुं कथंचन । १८ ।

अथ जयसिंह(हे)न झालाख्यो वरसाभिधः ।
प्रेषितो मि (मे)लनं कर्तुं तेनोक्तं मार्गगामिना । १९ ।
द(ले)लख(खा)न(नं) प्रत्येवं भवान्दिल्लीशमानितः ।
सहस्त्राण्यश्ववाराणां संगे पंचदशात्र ते । २० ।
राणेन्द्रस्यैको राजन्यो घट्टं रुद्ध्वा स्थितो भवान् ।
निः सरत्व(त्वे) व निश्चिन्तो राणेंद्रस्य तव स्फुटम् । २१ ।
स्नेहस्तदत्रपर्यन्तमायातस्त्वमतः परम् ।
नयावे (बावे) नोच्यते चं (चे) त्तं घट्टान्निसारयाम्यहम् । २२ ।
उच्यते चेत्स्थापयामि नबावेन तदेरितम् ।
पश्चात्सैन्यं समायाति मास्तु तेनापि वारणम् । २३ ।
घट्टत्रयस्य मार्गस्य दृष्ट्यर्थं प्रेषिता भटाः ।
तैरुक्तं तु नबावेन कृतं घट्टत्रयं दृढम् । २४ ।
ततो न निसृतस्तत्र नबावस्तदनन्तरम् ।
सहस्त्ररूप्यमुद्रास्तु दत्वै (त्वै) कस्मै द्विजातये । २५ ।
अग्रेसरं च कृत्वा तं नबावो रणकेसरी ।
निस्सृतोऽन्येन मार्गेण रात्रौ तत्रापि सैन्यवान् । २६ ।

रत्नसी रावतो रत्नं ये (यो) धाना(नां) मार्गतो जवात् ।
रं(र)णं चक्रे निःसरणं नबावः का(क) ष्टतो व्यधात् ।२७।
इत्थं वलेलखानस्तु नि(:) सृतोय(घ) घट्टतः छलात् ।
दिल्लीशान्तिक आयातः पृष्टो दिल्लीश्वरेण सः । २८ ।

11. Diler Khan's Report to Aurangzeb.

(Canto XXIII, verses 29-31)

त्वं निस्सृत्य किमायातो राणकस्यानुयोगतः
वलेलखां तवोवाच नान्नं लब्धं मया प्रभोः । २९ ।
राणेन्द्रो मम पश्चात्तु हंतुं मां समुपागतः ।
योधा मे मारितास्तेन नानाऽहं तेन निःसृतः । ३० ।
अन्नाभावान्नित्यमेव लोकानां तु चतु(:)शता (ती) ।
मृताहं निःसृतस्तस्माच्छ्रुत्वा दिल्लीश आकुलः । ३१ ।

12. Negotiation through Shyam Singh.

(Canto XXIII, verses 32-33.)

अथाकबर आयातो मि(मे) ल नं कर्तुमुद्यतः ।
राणाश्रीकर्णसिंहस्य द्वितीयस्तनयो बली । ३२ ।
गरीबदासस्तत्पुत्रः श्यामसिंह इहागतः ।
कृं (कृ)त्वा मि(मे)लनवार्ता(र्तां) तां परावृत्य गतो वृद्धाम् ।३३।

13. Conclusion of Peace.

(Canto XXIII, verses 34-62.)

ततो दिलेरखानस्तु मिलने दार्ढ्यमातनोत् ।
तथा हसन्नलीं खां च मिलनस्य विधिं व्यधात् । ३४ ।
जयसिंहोथ मिलनं कर्तुमुद्योगमातनोत् ।
श्रीमद्राजसमुद्रस्य अग्रभागे स्थितस्ततः । ३५ ।

सहस्राण्यश्ववाराणां सप्त स सप्तकतिविषाम् ।
मध्ये स्थितः सप्तसप्तिसमतेजाः समाबभौ । ३७ ।

पदातीनामयुतकं संगे स्थापितवान्प्रभुः ।
तदा पत्तिमयं प्रोक्तं जगद्दृष्ट्वा (ध्रु) वं जनैः । ३८ ।

महाशौर्यो महाधैर्यो जयसिंहस्ततो बली ।
झालेंद्रं चन्द्रसेनाख्यं चोहानं स्थापयन्पुरः । ३९ ।

रावं सबलसिंहाख्यं परमारशिरोमणिम् ।
वैरीसालं महारावं राठोरान्वीरठक्कुरान् । ४० ।

चौडावतान्रणे चंडान् शक्तान्शक्तवतांस्तथा ।
राजा रानावताजेयान्राजन्यान् जन्यदुर्जयान् । ४१ ।

सर्वान्स वर्वरानाढ्यान् संगे संस्थाप्य सोत्सवः ।
राणेन्द्रों रणदुर्धर्षो मिलनार्थी मुदाचलत् । ४२ ।

रक्तध्वजैः शोभमाना भांति नाना मदद्विपाः ।
सपल्लवद्रुमा गोत्रा एकत्र स्थापिताः किमु । ४३ ।

वैरिग्राहगणे(णं)महीधरकुलैः सद्रत्नवृन्दैरहो
राजचक्रचयैश्च(?)वडवास्फूर्जित्प्रतापैर्वृतः ।
उद्योगिभीवरोयहिभोगिनिवहैयपावयापूर्वयो (?)
गाम्भीर्येणयुतो विराजति जयो राणाऽर्णवः किं परम् ।४४।

औरंगजेबवीरस्य दिल्लीशस्य सुतस्य सः ।
जगत्प्राणसुरत्राणआजमस्य प्रतापिनः । ४५ ।

आज्ञया निशतासिंधु गा(गां)भीर्यगुणसागरः ।
दिल(ले)लखां महावीरो हसन्नाज वपूरितः । ४६ ।

तथा हरा(स) अल्लीखां अन्येऽपि म्लेच्छभूभुजः ।
राणेंद्रो रायसिंहाख्योरत्तलामपुरस्थितः । ४७ ।

हाडाकिशोरसिंहाख्यो गौडभूपस्तथापरे ।
हिंदू(हिन्दू) म्लेच्छमहावीरा आयाता संमुखं सुखान् । ४८ ।

दिल्लीपतीयैः स्वीयैश्च देशपालः समावृतः ।
जयसिंहो विभावाजौ दिक्पालैर्मघवा वृतः । ४९ ।

ततः श्रीजयसिंहाख्यपूर्वोक्तैष्ठ क्कुरैर्वृतः ।
गरीबदासनाम्नः स्वपुरोहितवरेण वा । ५० ।

भी(भू) प्रथां(था)नवै(श्यै)न युक्ते(क्तः) सुयोनितेजसा ।
महाभाग्यो(महा)शौर्यो महोत्साहो महामनाः ।५१।

हि(हिं)दुम्लेच्छमहावीरदेशनाथविशोभितः ।
आजमाख्यसुरत्राणमणेर्दर्शनमातनोत् । ५२ ।

आजमाख्यसुरत्राणो राणेंद्रस्यादरं भृशम् ।
अकरोद्विनयोपेतस(स्स) स्नेहमनुदर्शयन् । ५३ ।

एकादशगजानश्वांश्चत्वारिंशन्मितान्शुभान् ।
आजमाख्यराने(णें)द्रोप (?) यामास सुदर्पान् । ५४ ।

आजमाख्यसुरत्राण एकं मदालसं द्विपम् ।
अष्टाविंशतिसंख्याश्वान्सहेमवसनत्रयीम् । ५५ ।

पंचाशत्प्रमिता भूषः(षाः)समूहं रानभूभुजे ।
ददौ महानन्दमयमिलनं त्वनयोरभूत् । ५६ ।

दलेलखां तदोवाच सुलतान शृणु प्रभो ।
अयं वीरचन्द्रसेनो राना झालशिरोमणिः । ५७ ।

रावः सवलसिंहोयं रत्नसीनाम रावतः ।
चोण्डावता रणे चं(च)डाः शप्ताः(क्ताः) शक्तावतास्तथा ।५८ ।

परमाराश्च राठोडास्तथा राणावतोत्तमाः ।
रणेसिंहाः पर्वतेषु मार्गं येदवुरुत्तमाः । ५९ ।

युयुधुर्मे महायोधा ज्ञातव्यं विजिताबु(बु)धे ।
दिल्लीशेन पराक्रान्ता रानोक्त्या रक्षितुं ध्रुवम् । ६० ।

आजमा(मो)प्युक्तवानेवं सत्यमेवं न संशयः ।
संतुष्टो जयसिंहोऽथ ददावाज्ञां कृतादरः । ६१ ।

जे(ज)यसिंहो महाभाग्यो वी(रः) शिबिरमागतः ।
अस्यासी(द्भाग्य)तः शीघ्रं मिलनं गजतावरात् (?) । ६२ ।

The text of the inscription reproduced here is based on the text as in *Vir Vinod,* in the *Epigrahia Indica* edition of the text and my own text as printed (but not published) for the Punjab University Oriental Publications Fund. I have tried to correct the scribe's misspellings and reconstruct the text where possible.

APPENDIX III

English Translation from Ranchhod.

1. Shah Jahan's attack on Chitor.

Canto VI, verses 11-26.

In the year 1711, in the month of Āsvayuj, king Rajasimha having heard that Shah Jahan, the lord of Delhi, had arrived in Ajmer, and that Saddullah Khan, the minister of the lord of Delhi, had arrived in Chitrakuta, sent Bhatta Madhusudana to his presence (11-12).

The Telang (Brahmana) of Kathodi family went to the Khan. The Khan, regarding him as Pandit, inquired as to why the Rana had recalled Gharib Das as well as Jhala Rai Simha.

The Bhatta replied that this had happened from the very beginning. Sakta Simha, intrepid in battle, the brother of Rana Pratap, and the Ravata Megha by name having come from Mewar, had been fixed up by the lord of Dilli, but then (both of them) returned to Mewar. So, God has created two places for the Kshatriyas employed by their master. (13-17).

The Khan said, "This is true." Then the Khan again remarked, "Well, Pandit, tell me the number of horsemen of the Rana." (18). The Bhatta replied, '(it is) twenty thousand.' He (then) said, "the number of horsemen of the lord of Dilli is a lac. Then how do you equate (the two) ?" The Bhatta replied, "listen Khan, clearly. The equality of the one lac horsemen of the lord of Dilli with twenty thousand of Rana has been established by the Creator (himself)." Then the Khan, who was inwardly angry, spoke thus. "If the Rana's son, (Jai Singh) accompanied by Khan, sees Shah Jahan, he shall be granted, by the lord of Dilli, (at my recommendation) fourteen regions (cities ?)" (19-22)." Thus the devoted servant of the master, Madhusudan, the maker of a great speech, rendered a service to the Rana (23).

Rajasimha having considered that the sons of his ancestors had met in company with the sons of the lord of Dilli, sent his senior son Sultansimha, together with Thakuras, in the company of Darasakoha, son of Shah Jahan (24 and 25). Thus the king, Rajasimha, who resembled Vikramaditya in performing sacred rituals, in charity and valour, made friends with Shah Jahan. (26)

2. Marriage of Bhava Simha Baghela and the raising of the status of Baghelas.

Canto VIII, verses 37-43.

In the year 1721, in the month of Margasirsa, on the 8th lunar day of the dark fortnight, King Rajasimha having arranged and given away according to proper rites, his daughter Ajavakumvari to prince Bhavasimha, son of the Baghela King Bhupasimha, lord of Bandhogarh, gave (in marriage) 98 maidens of his relatives to various high chiefs. (37-39).

King Rajasimha of special splendour, seated in the kitchen, with the Ksatriyas of Bandhogarh (including) prince Bhavasimha, with whom dining was prohibited, shone forth, while taking his food. The Ksatriyas from Bandhogarh, then, said, "The exceedingly purifying food of Rana Rajasimha is undoubtedly the food of the holy favour of Jagannatharaya. Today we who are eating that food have been purified. The king then gave horses, elephants and ornaments to the bridegrooms. (40-43).

3. Jaisimha's mission to Delhi.

Canto XXII, verses 1-6.

When the year 1735 had expired, on the 11th lunar day of the bright fortnight of (the month of) Chaitra, the hero, Jayasimha, set out at the instance of Shri Rajasimha, and this Maharajakumara arrived at Ajmer. (1-2).

In order to see Aurangzeb, the lord of Dilli, he started for Dilli, and this prince Jaya marched protected by his troops. (3). In an excellent camp two Kosas from Dilli, he met the lord of Dilli, who did him honour. (4). He (the emperor) gave him (Jayasimha) a pearl necklace, the ornament for the chest, brocades, a lordly elephant adorned with raiments, and similar lofty horses (5). (The emperor) gave brocades and horses to Chandrasena named Jhala, and to the priest Gharib Das of excellent name (6).

4. War in Mewar.

Canto XXII, verses 10-25.

When the year 1736 had elapsed, on the eleventh lunar day of the dark fortnight of (the month of) Pausha, the lord of Dilli arrived in Mewar. (10).

First, his son named Akbar and (also) Tahavar Khan, arrived with the army. There in the beautiful Rajanagar, their men committed crimes against the royal temple. (11-12.)

There Sakta, the best of the Saktavatas, son of the Puravata Sabal Simha and brother of Mohan Singh, fought a terrible battle. (13).

A certain brave warrior Chomdavata and twenty-five soldiers, having given battle, departed for heaven, after piercing the region of the Sun (14).

"Let, the hosts of exalted heroes, having made a resolve, come at my bidding, with guns and shot, in order to fight" and at the Rana's words that happened. (15-16).

Then came the lord of Dilli to the great pass of Dahavari, having brought about the fall of its entrance. (17).

He stayed here for 21 days and then on one night, secretly reached the wonderful (city of) Udayapur ; this is the oracle. (18).

At that time Akbar also reached the great city of Udayapura, as also Tahavar Khan, and their soldiers performed their duty (19).

Then, perchance, Akbar went to see Ekalinga, and having seen the passes of Amberi and Cirava, came back to camp. (20).

Jhala Pratapa, resident of Kamketapura, having seized two elephants from the army of the lord of Dilli, presented them to the lord Rana. (21)

(The people) called Valla, staying at Bhadesar, brought to the master (i.e. the Rana), a pack of horses, a herd of elephants, and a string of camels, when he was staying at Nainwara. (22).

In that manner fifty thousands of men were lost. The lord of Dilli then reached Chitrakuta; and Akbar also came there having given out contrary publicity. So also came Hasan Ali Khan, from Chhappan. (23-24).

Then the lord Rana swelled with anger hastily came towards Nahin, from the village Kotadi, together with his army. (25).

5. Bhima in Gujarat.

Canto XXII, Verses 26-29.

Sent by the king Rana, prince Bhimsimha, destroyed Ida and Said Khan fled from there. (26).

Badnag was plundered, and Bhimsimha here took forty thousand silver coins as penalty (27).

In Ahmadnagar (Ahmedabad) the great hero Bhimasimha obtained two lacs of silver coins and caused the goods to be looted..

One big mosque, and three hundred small mosques were destroyed by Bhimasimha giving vent to his ire produced by the destruction of temples (29).

6. Jaisimha's Exploits

Canto XXII, Verses 30-48.

The wise and eager Maharajakumara Jayasimha, by the order of Rana, the great lord of the earth, marched towards Chitrakuta, taking with him, Chandrasena, (also) called Jhala, the Chauhan army leader Rao Sabalasimha, (who was) wise in fighting, shining in the company of his brother Rao Kesari Simha, Rathoda Gopinatha, son of Arisimha, Bhagavantasimha, and a host of blessed Ksatriyas; thirteen thousand horsemen, and twenty thousands of excellent infantry, in order to achieve success in his cherished objective. (30-35).

Then those greatly excited Thakkurs, fought during the night and killed a thousand men and three elephants, and the horses which they had brought, of the lord of Dilli. Akbar then retired. (36).

The warriors having captured fifty horses, brought them to prince Jayasimha, who became delighted. (37).

Then prince Jayasimha, who had performed his duty and who was successful in the great battle, saw the illustrious lord Rana. (38).

7. The Battle of Ghanora

Canto XXII, verses 39-44.

Gangakumvara, son of Saktāvata Rāvata Kesarisimhavarma who held the position of a prince, having captured eighteen intoxicated elephants and lines of horses and strings of camels from the army of the lord of Dilli, offered them to the Rana. (39-40).

Then the prince, Bhimasimha, accompanied by a force, having been deputed by the lordly Rana, fought a battle with Akbar and Tahavar Khan, which was like the battle between Indra and demons (41).

He who was comparable to Nala and possessed the valour for fighting, having passed by that great passage, Devasuri, fought a battle at the town of Ghanora. (42).

The Solanki hero, Bika, fought a battle for the protection of the pass. (43).

Then the prince Gajasimha, sent by the Rana, with a force, destroyed Begampur, that big (town) (44).

8. Aurangzeb's Overtures.

Canto XXII, Verses 45-46.

Aurangzeb, the lord of Dilli, then said "I have decided to make peace with the Rana either by surrendering three kingdoms or by giving 3 lacs of silver coins." What followed, either through fate or the (effect) of the Kali age, I shall narrate next. (45-46).

9. Jaisimha's Accession.

Canto XXIII, 9-10.

Then the victorious hero Jayasimha, encamped at the town of Kadaij. (9).

Having passed 15 days, the hero skilful in battle and the lord of Aksohini, occupied the throne of the Rana to protect the earth. (10).

10. Jaisimha's Engagement against the Mughals.

Canto XXIII, Verses 11-28.

When the year 1737 had expired, the high-minded Jayasimha, who illuminated the path of bravery, and who bestowed wealth on supplicants, while residing in the town of Kadaija, having heard that Tahavar Khan, had arrived having passed by Devasuri, and had transgressed the bounds of the pass, filled with rage, despatched his brother the terrible Bhimasimha. (11-13).

Having seen Bikasolanki and having heartened him, (made him) eager for that the highly terrible Bhimasimha and Bika ,the best of the Solankis, destroyed the Muslim armies, and Tahavar was held up for 8 days, and when released, he was lack-lustre like one released from Rahu. (14-15).

Jayasimha who had arrived in the vicinity of Ghanora (heard) that Diler Khan had arrived in the hills of the Chappan region, and that Rana's men having given him passages, he had come to Gogumda-ghatta. Then the pass was blocked by Rana's heroes who were famous in the world. Ravata Ratnasi too stood in the pass which was difficult to pass on account of stones. Then Diler Khan could not get away by any means. (16-18).

Jayasimha sent Varasa Jhala to meet him. En route, he said to Diler Khan, "You are honoured by the lord of Dilli. Here there are 15,000 horsemen with you. Only one noble of the Rana stands blocking the pass. You may get out without fear. The Rana obviously has kindly feelings for you. That is why you have come so far." Then the Nawab said this, "I shall get out of the pass. But if you say so, I shall hold. My army is coming behind. Let there be no obstruction by it." (19-23).

Soldiers were sent to examine the road to the three passes. They told the Nawab that the three passes were strongly guarded. (24).

Then the Nawab did not get out and afterwards having given a hundred coins to a certain Brahmin and making him the guide, the Nawab, the very lion in battle, went out at night by a different route. (25-26).

But even there, that jewel of warriors, Ravata, Ratansi possessing an army, quickly engaged him in action, and the Nawab could get out (only) with difficulty. (27).

Thus Nawab Khan got out of the pass by a trick. When he came to the lord of Dilli, the latter asked. (28).

11. Diler Khan's Report to Aurangzeb.

Canto XXIII, Verses 29-31.

Having been asked by the lord of Dilli, as to why he had returned, having come out and why the Rana was not pursued, Diler Khan replied, "Lord, I did not find food. (and) (29).

The King Rana came from behind to kill me. My warriors were killed by him. That is why I have returned. For want of food, 400 people died every day. That is why I have come out." Having heard that the lord of Dilli became perturbed (30, 31).

12. Negotiations through Shyam Singh

Canto XXIII, verses 32-33.

Then Akbar, ready to make peace, arrived. Shyamsingh, son of Gharibdas and the second brave son of Sri Rana Karanasimha, came here and having made a firm talk about peace, went back.

13. Conclusion of Peace.

Canto XXIII, verses 34-62

Diler Khan firmly advocated the making of peace, Hasan Ali Khan laid down the procedure for peace. (34).

Then Jayasimha too put forth efforts to make peace, and took up a position in front of the Rajasamunda. (34).

Standing amidst the 7,000 horsemen he stood like the sun among planets, and shone forth, equal in brilliance to the sun. (36).

When Jayasimha was seated on a horse, equal to that of the sun, people remarked, "The world appears as if consisting of horsemen (only)." (37).

That lord stationed with him. 10,000 foot-soldiers, then surely, the people having seen that, exclaimed that the world was made up of infantry. (38).

Then the hero Jayasimha of great valour and fortitude, placing in front the Chauhan lord Jhala Chandrasena by name, and Rao Sabalasimha, the crest-jewel of the Paramaras, the Maharao Vairisala, and the brave Thakkurs of the Rathor family, the Chundavatas, fierce in battle, as also the strong Saktavatas, the Ranavatas invincible in battle, and Ksatriyas, difficult to be conquered in fight; having taken into his company all those who were rich in great valour, that lord Rana, difficult to be overcome in battle, went out with joy and festivity. (39-42).

The several intoxicated elephants shining with the red banners looked splendid, as if the mountains with the trees with sprouts had been put at one place (43).

The victorious ocean-like Rana, surrounded by hosts of crocodiles in the form of enemies, with heaps of jewels in the form of royal clans, surrounded by hosts of troops whose glory shone like the submarine fire, with the officers called Bhogis, active like the great waves, and possessed of serenity, as if in their old tradition, shines; for who can excell him ? (44).

By the order of the glorious Sultan Azam, the son of Aurangzeb, the protector of the world and the lord of Dilli, the great hero Diler Khan who was a sea of wisdom and ocean of the virtue of profundity, laughing, full of joy, and so also Hasan Ali Khan, as well as other Muslim Khans, and Rathor named Ram Simha, who resided at Ratlam, Hada Kishor Simha, King of Gonda, as well as other great heroes—Hindus and Muslims, came face to face with ease. (45-48).

Jayasimha, surrounded by his own governors as well as those of the lord of Dilli, shone, in that contest, like Indra surrounded by the Lokapālas. (49).

Then the illustrious (Rana) accompanied by the eight Thakkuras named above, as also by his excellent Purohita Garibdas. (50).

Accompanied by Bhikhu, the chief of the merchants and bankers, who possessed the glory of high birth, the magnanimous, exceedingly brave and courageous, and very high-minded and looking splendid in the company of Hindu and Muslim brave kings, appeared before that jewel of a Sultan, called Azam. (51-52).

The Sultan, named Azam, possessed of humility showed great respect to the lordly Rana, showing great affection. (53).

The lordly Rana of exceeding pride, presented eleven elephants and forty horses to Azam. (54.).

Sultan Azam gave to Rana the king one elephant languid with intoxication, 28 horses together with three pieces of golden drapery, and 50 dresses. This was indeed a great meeting of the two. (55-56).

Then Diler Khan said, "Listen my lord the Sultan, this is Rana Jhala Chandrasena, the crest-jewel of brave, this is Rao Sabalasimha, this is Ravata Ratnasi; these are Chondavata warriors fierce in battle, and also the capable Saktavatas.

These are Paramaras and Rathoras, as also the excellent Ranavatas, who are lions in battle, who gave me passage in the hills. (57-59).

O, ocean of wisdom, please know that these great warriors fought against me, in order to protect, to be sure (their country) at the bidding of the Rana, (having been) attacked by the lord of Dilli. (60)."

Azam too remarked thus, "There is no doubt, it is true." Jayasimha who had been honoured and (was therefore) satisfied gave orders. (61).

The brave and magnanimous Jayasimha having arrived in his camp, fortunately his meeting was accomplished quickly. (62).

APPENDIX IV

The founder of Banera Raj

Maharana Raj Singh of Mewar had eight sons. The first two, Sultan Singh and Sardar Singh, predeceased their father.[1] Jai Singh, the third son, succeeded Rana Raj Singh at his death in 1680. The fourth son was Bhim Singh who first gained fame in the Rajput struggle against Aurangzeb and, after the conclusion of the peace, rose to eminence under Aurangzeb in the Deccan.

It is claimed by his descendants of the Banera Raj (in Mewar) that Bhim Singh and Jai Singh were born on the same day of different mothers and that Bhim Singh was born earlier. This was accepted by Tod[2] and later on by Kaviraj Shyamal Dass in his *Vir Vinod*[3]. A chronicle of Mewar written probably in the first half of the eighteenth century supports this tradition.[4] But the evidence on the other side is overwhelming, *Mirat-i-Ahmadi* calls him a younger son when speaking of his expedition to Gujarat in 1680.[5] Earlier we find from the *Ma'āsiri-'Ālamgīrī,* that in March 1679, the Maharana sent his eldest son Jai Singh as his representative to pay his respects to the emperor who had moved on to Ajmer immediately after hearing of Jaswant Singh's death.[6] It was customary to send the eldest son as the representative of the Maharana to the court, now and then, and the deputation of Jai Singh to the imperial court meant that he was at that time the heir-apparent. Further, the different collections of horoscopes as pointed out by MM. Gauri Shanker Ojha all indicate the same conclusion.[7] There

1. *Vir Vinod,* D. A. V. College transcript, 437.
2. *Tod,* 1, 316.
3. *Vīr Vinod,* 597.
4. *Udaipur Ki Khayāl* (MS), D.A.V. College transcript p. 12.
5. *Mīrāt-i-Ahmadī,* 1, 204.
6. *Ma'āsir-i-'Ālamgīrī* p. 173.
7. *History of Mewarī,* (Hindi), vol. II. p. 888.

does not seem to be any reason to disregard the combined weight of all these facts.

When peace had been made with Mewar, Auragzeb's officers were very anxious about Bhim Singh's submission.[8] But he was not to be found in Jai Singh's retinue, and Azam had to be content with Jai Singh's assurance that he knew nothing about him as he had quarrelled with him.[9]

But Aurangzeb was not prepared to let slip his opportunity. This quarrel between Bhim Singh and Jai Singh enabled him to lure Bhim Singh to his own service.

On 24th July, 1681 Bhim saw Daler Khan, the Mughal commander, who received him graciously and recommended to the emperor that he should be granted a jagir. On 29th July, 1681, Aurangzeb accepted this recommendation and conferred the Jagir of Bahera on Bhim Singh. On August 2, it was decided to call Bhim to court and Daler Khan was ordered to bring him to court himself. Daler Khan, however, excused himself and Bhim was sent to Ajmer with Muzaffar. On 11th August, Bhim was admitted to the imperial presence at Ajmer, the signal honour of sending the Bakshi and other high Mansabdars to meet him at the gates of the court being accorded to him. He was created a commander of 4,000 horse and 3,000 Jats and created a Raja. Of course presents were also showered on him. Further, he was asked to report himself daily in the private audience-chamber of the Emperor, the Ghusal Khana. However, on Friday no audiences were usually given and we find Raja Bhim's vakil asking for instructions on August 19, as to where his master should report himself on Friday. The Emperor was therefore pleased to order that Bhim should have audience even on Fridays when the Emperor was riding out. On August 16 Raja Bhim requested the Emperor to confer the Pargana of Mangrot as a Watan Jagir on him. He was asked to submit his application through the usual official channels. On the 17th Bhim's son Ajaib Singh and his cousin Fateh Singh had

8. *Vir Vinod*, 589.
9. *Jaipur Records*, vol. III, 87, *Vir Vinod* 591

audience and Ajaib Singh was awarded suitable gifts on August 21. Early on August 23, Raja Bhim's mother died and the Emperor ordered an officer of rank to go to his house and get the mourning terminated. This was done and on the 25 August, Raja Bhim paid his respects to the Emperor. On the 27th, he accompanied the Emperor to Pushkar and presented Rs. 2000 as a Nazr probably on account of his having received the patent for his Mansab. His earlier application for Mangrot having been rejected, he now requested for the grant of Mui Maidana. This again was refused as it was Jagat Singh's Jagir. Though a high Mansab was conferred on Raja Bhim, he was still impoverished. On Daler Khan's recommendations, Rs. 20,000 were granted to him on September 15, in order to enable him to tide over his difficulties. He was now left behind at Ajmer to help its viceroy, prince Azam. Bhim, however, was not very happy in his new command. He seems to have been kept at Ajmer merely as a watcher and though the Rathors were still in the field, he was not yet trusted enough to be sent against his whilom allies. While Aurangzeb was proceeding to the Deccan, he received a letter from Bhim which was discussed on October 13 in the court. He wanted to take an active part in the warfare of the times and had requested that he might be allowed to join the Emperor in the Deccan and given some active command there. Orders were issued, therefore, to a mace-bearer to bring Bhim to court after allowing him to spend a fortnight in his jagir. Bhim's efforts to get a suitable jagir for his maintenance now bore fruit and his vakil attached to the imperial court succeeded at last in getting Khairabad and Mui Maidana in jagir in exchange for Baran. It took, however, more than two months to get the regular Farman, which is dated December 24, 1681. Of course all this took time and we find Bhim still in Rajputana in November. On November 13, Rs. 1,000 were granted to him as his travelling allowance to the Deccan. His efforts to get some land as a Watan Jagir (irrevocable grant), meanwhile, bore fruit and on the same day Lolai was given to him as Watan Jagir. He was now allowed three months respite in his Jagir after which he was to leave for the Deccan. An imperial messenger was again told off to see to the execution of the imperial command. But Bhim Singh was not destined to reach the Deccan till August 11, 1686. Whether Bhim did not like to leave Rajputana or Aurangzeb thought his presence necessary there and cancelled his earlier instructions, it is difficult to decide. Bhim had audience on August 21, 1686 and was appointed to a suitable post in the army.[10] But he soon incurred imperial displeasure and his rank was reduced by 500. At the siege of Hyderabad, however, he displayed conspicuous valour. This resulted in an increment and he again became a commander of 4,000 horse[11].

He rendered very useful services against Marathas and the Shia States of the Deccan. In 1691, probably, his services were rewarded by an increment in his Mansab and the grant of a Jagir in Malpura in Jaipur. This opened up a very difficult chapter in the relations between the Rajas of Jaipur and Bhim Singh. The Kachhwahas did not like the Sasodias butting in on what they had regarded as their own preserve. Bhim kept his brother Dal Singh there; the revenue and civil administration were entrusted to one Dil Ram Brahman[12]. The Kachhwahas complained that neither Bhim nor his brother was keeping the requisite number of soldiers in the jagir. This led to a reduction in Bhim's Jagir though not probably in his Mansab. Towards the end of the year 1692 the contested territory was divided between Bhim and Raja Bishan Singh; but this did not ease the situation[13]. Both sides went on making claims and counter-claims and heavily bribed the Mughal officers concerned, especially Bahram Khan.[14] Bhim, who was serving at that time in the army of Mu'izz-ud-Din, probably had suffered a set-back early in the year 1692. Aurangzeb had prohibited the public celebration of Hindu festivals. These orders were enforced strictly even in the camp. Bhim, however, along with certain

10. This is mostly based on the daily records of Aurangzeb's reign. Whenever a date is given the statement is based on the record of the same date.

11. *Zawābat-i-'Ālamgiri* (MS), f. 163 b.

12. *Jaipur Records*, vol. XI, pp. 84-87.

13. *Jaipur Records*, vol. VIII, vol. XI 91, 113, 200 pp. 19, 21 and 22, 44-49; 94, 95, 107-112.

14. *Jaipur Records*, vol. XI, p. 200.

other Hindu Rajas, celebrated the Holi festival. The censor accompanying the expeditionary force tried to stop the celebration, but in vain. He complained to the emperor and on April 1, 1692, the case came up for imperial orders. Of course nothing could be done, but the emperor gave orders that in future the prohibition should be strictly enforced.[15] Naturally the emperor was displeased with Bhim, and this might have given the Kachhwahas a chance for creating trouble against him. But Bhim was a great warrior. The emperor could not afford to be displeased with him for long; and on May 8 he was appointed to command an expedition on his own.[16] The cause of the Kachhwahas received further help on account of the appointment of Bishan Singh against the Jats. This Kachhwaha-Sasodia struggle continued with varying fortunes for some time, ending in favour of the Kachhwahas with the death of Bhim Singh in 1694.

Bhim died in August 1964 in the Deccan, while serving in Bedar Bakht's army. One of his Ranis, daughter of Padma Singh, burnt herself to death on her husband's funeral pyre though an attempt was made to dissuade her. Of his sons the eldest at this time was Suraj Mal who, unfortunately, was absent in Rajputana, getting married. He was appointed a commander of 1,000 on the 26th of August, 1694.[17] On Bedar Bakht's recommendation, on September 19, 1694, mansabs were conferred on Bhim's sons. Sujan Singh became a commander of 300, Ajab Singh of 300, whereas Suraj Mali's personal command was raised to 900 horse.[18] Zorawar Singh, another son of Raja Bhim, had audience on April 3, 1703.[19] Bije Singh, another son, was appointed a three-sadi on August 23, 1703[20].

15. *Imperial Court Bulletins*, dated April 1, 1697.
16. Ibid; dated May 8, 1692.
17. Ibid; dated August 8, 94; The date given in *Ma'āsir-i-'Alamgiri* which is equivalent to January 7, 1694 is wrong. The death was reported on 26th August, 1694; it could not have occurred seven months earlier. A letter from Bhim was read in the court on July 17, 1694 (vide Newsletter of that date).
18. Ibid; dated 18th September, 1694.
19. Ibid, dated April 3, 1703.
20. Ibid, dated August 23, 1703.

Raja Bhim Singh was a great warrior. He served Mewar faithfully till the treaty of peace between the Mughals and Mewar. His courage and bravery won for him the signal honour of becoming a commander of 4,000 horse at his entry into the Mughal service, with the title of Raja. He served the Mughals faithfully in the Deccan and, despite his religious prejudices, Aurangzeb raised his command to 5,000 horse, so pleased was he with his work. His career in the Deccan goes against the commonly accepted belief that, after the war in Rajputana in 1680, the Rajputs ceased to serve in the Mughal armies. Here was Bhim Singh, their toughest opponent in Rajputana, enlisting himself under the Mughal banner and serving Aurangzeb faithfully.

CHAPTER IX

Raj Singh and His Times

Born on 24 September 1929, Raj Singh was just 52 when he died on 22 October, 1680. He had succeeded his father on 10 April 1652, when he was a young man of hardly twentyfour. As was usual among the ruling princes at the time, he was a much married man, having married as many as eighteen wives. From them he had 9 sons and one daughter[260]. Soon after his accession—how soon we cannot determine—he had to face, it is said, a very serious palace intrigue. He had two sons, Sultan Singh and Sardar Singh when he came to the throne. The eldest, Sultan Singh, could not have yet entered his teens when the mother of the second son, desiring, it is said, to secure the throne for her son Sardar Singh, poisoned her husband's mind against him. In a fit of ungovernable fury, Raj Singh, procured Sultan Singh's death. Sardar Singh's mother then tried to get her husband poisoned in order to hasten the accession of her son Sardar Singh, probably with an eye at securing the regency for herself. She had hatched this plan with a purohita. Somehow or other, the plan miscarried, the purohita and the Rani were both killed on the plan leaking out. Sardar Singh who could not have been yet in his teens committed suicide. Bard Udai Bhan, was saucy enough to comment adversely on Raj Singh whereupon he was killed. All this we are told happened some time before 1660 when the plan for Rajasamund was taken in hand.[261]

Though he had escaped this alleged death by poison, it seems he was fated to die poisoned. There is a veiled

260. *Vir-Viond*, II, 474-75.
261. Ibid, II, 446.

hint in the local tradition that on account of his determination to continue fighting against Aurangzeb, he was poisoned by parties opposed to prolonging the war. He died of poison at Aura, while on his way to Kumbalgarh.[262] This could hardly have been done at the instigation of his eldest son and successor, Jai Singh, who, we are told in a letter in Jaipur Records, had already been vested with full powers and formally proclaimed Rana.[263] Jai Singh's accession, as we have already seen in the last chapter, did not result in any slackening of Mewar's effort against Aurangzeb either.

Raj Singh and the Mughal Emperors.

Raj Singh had to pass the twentyeight years of his life facing heavy odds. He was twice embroiled with the Mughal emperors. On both occasions the quarrel had not been of his own seeking. Shah Jahan sent the largest Mughal force against Mewar in 1654 in order, so he proclaimed, to force Mewar to keep the terms of its treaty with Delhi. The alleged violations of this treaty had mostly taken place during his father, Jagat Singh's reign. Shah Jahan had challenged Raj Singh within less than a year of recognising him formally as the Rana of Mewar. Raj Singh had, as we have already seen, bidded his time then and made peace with the Mughals who had demolished the additions to their strengthening work at Chitor.

His chance came when Aurangzeb rebelled against his father. Without committing himself irrevocably to Aurangzeb's side before he had finally defeated his father and imprisoned him, Raj Singh entered upon protracted negotiations with him during Aurangzeb's rebellion. A Mewar mission was there to congratulate him when Aurangzeb crowned himself; Raj Singh secured the return of the additional territories which Shah Jahan had sequestered in 1654, before he had sent any armed forces to fight on behalf of Aurangzeb against his brothers. There is no reason to suppose that this force was any bigger than the contingent which Mewar had undertaken to supply in its treaty with Jahangir.

262. Ibid, II 473, 74.
263. *Jaipur Records, XIII,* 72-74.

Raj Singh, however, was not afraid of rubbing the Mughal emperors the wrong way when the Rajput tradition called for it. When the call from Charumati of Rupnagar came to save her from being married to a Muslim even though he was the emperor of India, Raj Singh did not hesitate and hastened to Rup Nagar to marry the princess. Again when Aurangzeb imposed the Jizya, Raj Singh entered a vigorous protest and almost challenged the emperor to realize it from him. Aurangzeb's attempt at incorporating Jodhpur in the royal dominions after the death of Maharaja Jaswant Singh might have been considered by a lesser man as the settling of an old score against a rival Rajput house which had been attacking Mewar interests ever since the days of Rao Maldev. But Raj Singh read it for what it was, an imperial claim against Rajput states whenever the occasion afforded a chance. The resulting Mewar-Marwar alliance almost shook the throne of the emperor and led to the only princely rebellion in Mughal history inspired by outside interests, abortive though this rebellion was.

His Military Strategy and Tactics.

That he was not only a great diplomat but a great military leader as well, Raj Singh proved in his conduct of the war against the Mughals. His illustrious predecessor Pratap had initiated the scorched earth policy in fighting the enemy. But the tactics of attacking the Mughals in their own territories and to face Mughal vandalism in Mewar and Marwar with an almost equally vicious vandalism of his own in Gujarat, Idar and elsewhere was a contribution of his own which made him a realist in medieval Hindu warfare, no longer bound to practise the art of war in the traditional s.yle. Again Pratap before him had refused to honour the much invoked call to a Rajput to fight to death and had adopted the strategy of not staking his all on the outcome of a single battle. He had preferred to fight a long drawn out war on his own where he could utilize all the advantages which nature could afford him in his own land. After his death three generations of Mewar rulers had lived life of ease unparallelled in the history of Mewar and there was a danger that such a tradition might be soon forgotten. In his war against Aurangzeb Raj Singh not only revived it but infused a new life and vigour in it rendering the Mughal commanders helpless against a foe whom they could not always locate. At the end of the war in his successor's reign the honours could be claimed to have been almost equally divided.

Patronage of literature.

Raj Singh was a great patron of letters. His reign is famous for a large number of literary works, which seemed to have been inspired by his active patronage. We have already noticed the most famous of them, the *Rājapraśasti Mahākāvyam.* Several other histories were written in his reign. Ranchhod himself wrote *Amara Kāvya.* Sadāśiva wrote *Rājaratnākara.* Dhundirāja also produced another work with the same title. Mān wrote *Rāja Vilāsa* in Hindi verse covering Raj Singh's reign. A *Vaṁśāvali* was brought together by Gopal Dās in Hindi and Sadashiva brought together a collection of Praśastis in his *Praśastisaṅgraha. Vaṁśāvali Rānāji, Sisod Vaṁśāvali* and *Sūryanainī* Chronicles seem to have been compiled in his reign. Lal Bhat wrote 101 adulatory verses about Raj Singh in his *Rājasiṁhaprabhāvarṇanam.*[264]

His Buildings.

Raj Singh was a great builder himself. His reign saw several buildings raised in Mewar. His queen Ramras Devi had a *Baoli* built near Debari.[265] The chief queen Charumati had a *Baoli* built at Rajnagar the same year. It cost Rs. 30,000.[266] Gobind Ram Vyas probably built another *Baoli* at Bhawani.[267] His chief minister, Dayal Das, had a Jain temple built on the hill opposite Nauchauki at Rajnagar and installed four Jain images there.[268]

264. *Bibliography* of A. R. G. Tiwari's unpublished thesis on maharana Udai Singh; *Bibliography of Medieval Rajas,* G.N. Sharma.

265. Inscription on the site.

266. Ranchhod, XIV, 11, 12.

267. Bhavana Baoli inscription on the site.

268. Inscription on the site.

The Maharana himself was responsible for adding several structures. In 1659 he put up a wall spanning the Debari pass keeping a door for passing in and out of the pass.[269] This was dictated by military needs. At Udaipur he extended the lake by excavating another tank Rangagar in 1668 and joining it with the waters surrounding the palace.[270] Another tank was excavated near the village Bari and named after his mother Jana Devi, Jana Sāgar. It is reported to have cost Rs. 688,000 including the donations given.[271] He built a new temple of goddess Amba, a local name in which Durga is remembered here.[272] He was not a narrow sectarian and proved it by building another temple dedicated to Krishna near Kankroli as the lord of Dwarka.[273] Mewar rulers had been paying visit to Dwarka in Gujarat and it was but appropriate that there be a temple dedicated to the god. The construction of Rajsamund was preceded by the building of a palace there,[274] near where later on the city of Raj Nagar came to be. He got the dam of Indrasar tank repaired.[275] As we have already seen, the building of the dam to produce the lake cost a very large amount of money. It is doubtful whether any medieval ruler of India had spent such a large amount of money for purposes of public welfare not even the greatest of the Grand Mughals. Certainly not one of them had spent such a large proportion of his resources for such a beneficial purpose.

Government and Administration.

Mewar under Raj Singh was governed in the traditional Rajput fashion. The Maharana was the head of the government in theory as well as in fact, even though in form he was a deputy—Diwan—of the god Ekaliṅga. This did not in any way affect his authority nor did it render the State a theo-

269. Ranchhod, VII, 26 to 28.
270. Ibid, VIII, 51, 52.
271. Ibid, VIII, 46 to 50.
272. Inscription on the site,
273. Ranchhod V, 1.
274. Ibid XVII,16
275. Ibid, X, 40-42.

cracy. It simply paid a tribute to the god who was supposed to have helped Bapa Rawal in founding the Guhil rule at Chitor.[276] We hear of Chief Ministers Dosi Bhiku, Fateh Chand and Dayal Das and Purohita (royal priest) Gharib Das as taking part in the affairs of the government. Rao Kesari Singh of Solambra is spoken of as a high personage at court who was present in the mandap when the consecration ceremony of Rajsamund was performed and who had himself weighed against silver.[277] He is also mentioned by Mān as one of the members of the council of war which considered the plan of the campaign against Aurangzeb.[278] The heads of the house of Solambra were supposed to occupy the first place among the Thakurs of Mewar on account of the fact that they represented the eldest son of Lakha, Chonda, who had renounced his claim to the throne. But Kesari Singh did not represent the senior Chundavat branch of the royal house. He had been given Solambra by Raj Singh who had sequestered it from Raghunath Singh.[279] Ranavat Ram Singh also seems to have occupied a high place in the administration; he is mentioned in the *Rājapraśasti* as entrusted with the supervision of the work at the dam. He was also present in the council of war.[280] Ranavat Maha Singh seems to have shared the supervision of the construction with Ranavat Ram Singh. Several Sahs are mentioned as participating in the work. Their function seems to have probably been confined to the financial supplies. Of these Sah Som Chandar is described as Vittagara, finance minister and accountant general rolled into one.[281] Purohita Gharib Das is not only present in the mandap at the time of the consecration ceremony, he is invariably present when matters of war or peace have to be discussed and carried through. A honorofic office was that of Devalia Diwan which the head of the house of Devalia bore to commemorate the fact that,

276. Local tradition.
277. Cf. above, Chapter on consecration.
278. Cf. chapter on Rajput War.
279. Ranchhod, XIV, 5, 6.
280. See above.
281. Cf. addenda at the end of the last slab.

when during the siege of Chitor by Bahadur Shah of Gujarat Vikramajit evacuated the fort to seek safety elsewhere, the then head of the house of Devalia, Rawat Bhag Singh was acknowledged as the Rana and invested with all the insignia of the Ranas of Mewar.[282] The present head of the Devalia house, Jhala Jai Singh was present at the council of war held to plan the campaign against the Mughals and is mentioned among the several commanders leading Mewar armies against the Mughals. He was also a member of the mission sent by Jai Singh to Azam to negotiate peace with the Mughals.[283]

Kesari Singh is also mentioned as one who had himself weighed against silver at the time of the consecration of the dam.[243] He seems to have occupied a high place at court. A very early inscription of the tenth century A.D. speaks of a several ministers serving the rulers of Mewar : Amātya, the chief minister, Sāndhivigrahika, the foreign minister, Akṣapaṭalika, the finance minister, Bamdapati, the chief bard and Bhiṣagadhirāja the chief physician.[285] We have all these officers, except that of the chief physician, functioning under Raj Singh. Three Pradhans, chief ministers, have been mentioned above, the Vittgara was the finance minister. Gharibdas seems to have fitted into an office corresponding to that of the foreign minister. Barhata Kesari Singh was the chief bard. As correspondence with other Hindu rulers was usually carried on in Sanskrit, we have a Sanskrit Secretary functioning in the state. He was known as Shastri. The office was hereditary.[286]

Besides these officials various important chiefs who held Jagirs under the Maharana also functioned as a sort of advisory council which met on certain ceremonial occasions.

282. *Harinangal Prabandh* of Yogiraj cited by A.R. Tiwari in his unpublished thesis.

283. See above.

284. See above.

285. Sarangeswar temple inscription of Allat, cited by Gauri Shankar Ojha, *Udaipur*, I, 122. Ahad inscription in Gauri Shankar, Ojha Udaipur I, 124 and 125.

286, Gauri Shankar, II, 444 (21).

They owed attendance at the capital at the time of Dasahra at least every year. When the war against Aurangzeb was decided upon, chiefs of Dilwara, Bijolia, Baigun, Solambar, Badnor, Parsoli, Bhindar, Kotharya, Dungarpur, Gogunda and Gharair are mentioned as participating therein. Chiefs of Anter, Bansi, Sardargarh, Sadri, Khairbad, Kailva, Sanvad, Lasani, Rupnagar, Nimri, Hinta, Bhadu trace their ancestory back to the days of Raj Singh. The royal princes of age and the brothers of the Maharana were also counted among the chiefs.

Thikanas and Jagirs.

The Jagirs provided an administrative machinery as well as a military force. The Jagirdars were administrators of the areas they held. But in the traditional and custom-bound society of the period, there was not much administration to be done. At the time of Dasahra all of them were bound to attend court for a period of 3o days, reaching capital 10 days before the commencement of the Dasahra. They were further bound to be present at the court for a stipulated period every year—probably for about three months.[287] During this period they were attended by their soldiers, probably leaving one half of them in their Jagirs.[288] They paid a tribute to the Maharana which was customarily supposed to be 1/6 of that income. Some of them enjoyed the privilege of giving asylum to those seeking their protection.[289] This was a discretionary 'right' arising out of the current notions of chivalry and seems to have been almost unlimited. It could sometimes degenerate into the chiefs almost becoming protectors and participators in the proceeds of robberies, thefts, and other offences committed by those whom they were supposed to protect. On succession to his 'Thikana', the new chief paid a 'nazrana' which varied with the income it was supposed to produce. Since the days of Rana Amar Singh, the Sardars were allowed to keep their Thikanas and the neighbouring villages, the rest of the villages were changed from time to time.[290] The change was usally affected when a new Jagirdar

287. *Treaties, Sanads and Engagements* edited by Archison, III, 43, 44.
288. Ibid, 45 to 47.
289. Ibid, 45 to 47.
290. Vir Vinod, II, 780, 788, 790.

assumed authority. It is necessary to remember that most of the chiefs were recent creations—usually dating from Rana Raimal's reign, if not later. The right of the Maharana to confiscate a Jagir or to transfer one holding for another was not much challenged in Mewar.

Royal Charities and Public works.

There was not much distinction between the Rana's household staff and administration. Works of public welfare were considered to be acts of personal piety of the ruler. Thus buildings, tanks, and wells were not looked after by officers of a public works department. Grants to scholars, Brahmans, bards and other men of piety were again personal decisions of the ruler and required no clearance from an ecclesiastical or a finance department.

Administration of Justice.

Administration of justice concerned the state as such occasionally. The village and caste panchayats decided most of the cases on their own knowledge of the parties or the issues involved. The civil law followed the *Yājñavalkya* Smṛti as expounded by Mitākṣarā whereas the customary law was found wanting.

Land Tenures.

Land was held by the ruler, the Jagirdars, the Bhumiyas and in charity.[291] The ruler charged one half of the produce from his tenants in the "Khalsa"; the jagirdars were held to charge the same from those who cultivated the land under them.[292] Some land was held for military service, some was given to civil administrators, even when they did not normally perform any military duties. Shasan land was held in charity, by Brahmans, Charans, scholars, temples, priests of places of worship, even by Sannyasis and 'beggars'.

291. This continued till recent changes in the law.
292. *Treaties*, III, 45-47.

Bhumi land was held by the descendants of the supposed original inhabitants of the villages. They were charged with the duty of safeguarding the village in which they held land. They paid a light tax on land, probably amounting to 1/6 of the produce and were further required to wait upon the Maharana's officers as and when they visited the neighbourhood or summoned them otherwise. When thus on duty they were paid a subsistence allowance usually in kind, sometimes in cash.

Other Levies.

Besides the payments made by those who held land, the state levied several other charges. Mandavi seems to have been a tax which was an amalgam of custom duty, octroi and sales tax—Mapa has usually been interpreted as octroi of a sort. Karivata was a tax on salt, how assessed we are not sure. Patasutriya was a tax on cloth. Chaukidari, pasturage rates, taxation on gambling, charges for providing armed escort to travellers and caravans levied both by the state as well as the local jagirdars through whose areas they passed formed other sources of revenue.[293] Occasionally fines were imposed usually for acts of insubordination or for what were then regarded as highly anti-social acts. It seems a small fee was paid for wood obtained from common forests.[294] As the Maharana was the supreme landlord, lands of Jagirdars, Bhumias, Shashan holders lapsed to him for failure of heirs. This however could have been only a very small source of revenue as adoption was current. Certain services imposed on the people saved the state expenditure and may as well be considered as impositions they had to bear. When the Maharana's army moved, it was the duty of the local people to supply forage for its animals and wood for the kitchens and canteens. When the ruler went on tour, he was similarly provisioned and part of his entourage had to be

293. Delwara temple inscription of 1491 V.S. in *Deva Mulapatak* 22, Abu inscription of 1506 in *Nagari Pracharani Sabha Patrika* S., I, 450-451

294. Nensi, II, 149.

supplied beddings and quilts in winters by the merchants, and bankers.[295] The state realized a royalty, on the working of the mines—iron, silver, copper, quarrying of marble.

Occasionally the inhabitants of a village were exempted from the payment of a tax.[296] This was an act of charity; presumably such grant of exemption once granted continued indefinitely. Sometimes some taxes or a part thereof were assigned for a religious service or a shrine[297].

A Multi-clan State.

Mewar was the foremost State of Rajputana. Its Sassodia ruler enjoyed the pride of place among all the Rajputs. But Mewar could not be called a 'Sassodia' state in the real sense of the term. Among its leading sardars in Raj Singh's time we have Rathors, Chauhans, Parmars, Solankis, and Kachhawahas. The descendants of Sassodias holding an important place in the state were mostly those descending from Rana Raimal in the sixteenth century.

Religion.

Though the ruler of Mewar has Shiva in his Lakulīśa form installed in the Ekaliṅga temple at Kailasapuri and the ruler is both his deputy and chief priest, this never made it a Shaivite state in any strict sense of the term. In Raj Singh's reign, things were not different. Royal piety as well as royal charity continued to be extended to the followers of all sects of Hindus, including Jains. As we have seen above, at the time of the consecration of the dam, the goddess earth, the gods of the clans, Gaṇeṣa, Varuṇa and Govinda were worshipped indifferently. Raj Singh himself had built a temple dedicated to Ambāmātā, another to Kṣṛṇa. Mewar does not seem to have been troubled with sectarian quarrels.

295. Tod, I, 170, 241.
296. Cf. Abu inscription cited above.
297. Cf. Delwara inscription cited above.

Social Organisation.

Hindus were divided in Mewar, as elsewhere in contemporary North India, among Brahmans, Kshatriyas, Vaishyas and Shudras. Mewar had however produced by now some peculiarities among some of these castes; Khatis, Pancholis, and Vohras among Brahmans, Pancholis among the Rajputs, and Pancholis and Kayasths among Vaishyas. Mewar had no equivalent of Khatris, bearing a label which is rather a vulgarized equivalent of Kshatri, but carrying on trade. Trade was in the hands of Jain Oswals and Hindu Mahajans who accepted their status as those of Vaishyas. The Rajputs in Rajputana claimed to be the true descendants of ancient Kshatriyas and even though the claim may be pronounced to be spurious to-day, it was accepted as true in the seventeenth century. Rajputs here formed the warrior class *par excellence*. Shudra was a label attached to those engaged in agriculture and handicrafts and others performing ministerial functions. From among them usually came the contemporary Das and Dasis, usually described as slaves but not bearing many of the disabilities which this class suffered in contemporary West. A dasi had even given a ruler to Mewar—Banbir about a hundred years ago[298].

The status of Shudras as well as of Dasas was not as low in Mewar as elsewhere because of the peculiar position the Bhils occupied in Mewar. They not only formed a recognized part of the Mewar army following its ruler, their participation was necessary in the coronation ceremony of every ruler of Mewar.[299]

Status of Women.

As the Rajapraśasti tells us when the consecration ceremony of the dam was performed, Maharana Raj Singh was accompanied by his chief Rani through the consecration ceremony. We learn elsewhere that the chief Rani used to

298. Banbir, one of the successors of Sanga.

299. Cf. Man's description of the Coronation of Raj Singh.

be present with the new Maharana at the time of the coronation of the Rana as well. Women thus seem to have occupied a higher place in Mewar than they did elsewhere in contemporay India[300].

300. Cf. the famous assertion of Tulsi Das that the drum, an animal, a shudra and a woman have the right to be beaten.

BIBLIOGRAPHY

I Rājapraśasti Mahākāvyam, Ranchhod. It has been described in the text and extracts reproduced in appendix II to the eighth chapter with their English translation in appendix III.

2. Rājvilās by Mān is an account of Raj Singh by a contemporary writer.

3-4. Chahār Chaman Brāhman and Inshāi-Brāhman by Chandar Bhan are useful as giving the account of his mission to Chitor by Chandar Bhan Brahman. The account from both the sources has been reproduced as an appendix to chapter 3. I have used the MS copies in Riza library, Muslim University Aligarh.

5. Vir Vinod by Shyamal Das (in Hindi) is a history of Rajputana, particularly of Udaipur State printed in 1887 in two volumes. It was 'published' only after 1947. It is useful as reproducing the original contemporary records about the reign of Raj Singh not available in original now.

6. Ādāb-i-Ālamgīrī, a collection of letters of and to Aurangzeb and also letters of Prince Akbar from the battlefield in 1680. I used the MS in Sir Jadunath Sarkar's Library, at Darjeeling. The collection has now been deposited in National Library, Calcutta.

7. Memoirs of Jahangir, English translation by Rogers.

8· Bādshāh Nāma by Waris (MS).

9. Nuskha-i-Dilkushā by Bhim Sen, a contemporary memoir of Aurangzeb's reign (MS).

10. Maāsir-i-Ālamgīrī by Muhammod S.M. Khan.

11. Muntkhib-ut Tawārīkh. As explained in my *Bibliography of Mughal India*, the account of Aurangzeb's reign here has been reproduced from Abul Fazl's Mamuri's account of Aurangzeb's reign.

12. Fatūhāt-i-'Ālamgīrī, Ishar Das (MS).

13. Kalimāt-i-Tayyibāt, (MS) Collection of Aurangzeb's letters.

14. Khatūt-i-Shivājī (MS).

15. Jaipur Records (MS).

16. Court Bulletins of Aurangzeb's Reign usually described as News letters of the Imperial Court (MS).

17. Ajītodaya (MS) Cited by Tiwari.

18. Rājrupaka (MS) Cited by Ran

19. Waqa's Ajmer.

I have cited the Persian MSS in sir Jodunath Sarkar's Library, now in the National Library Calcutta. I have described the MS work in my Bibliography of Mughal India.

MODERN WORKS

1. History of Udaipur (Hindi) Gaurishankar Hirachand Ojha.

2. History of Sarohi (Hindi), Gaurishankar Hira Chand Ojha.

3. Mewar and the Mughal Emperors, Gopinath Sharma.

4. Studies in Medieval India, Sri Ram Sharma.

5. Maharana Pratap, Sri Ram Sharma.

6. Bibliography of Mughal India, Sri Ram Sharma.

7. Annals of Rajasthan, James Tod.

8. Last Sack of Chitor, Sri Ram Sharma in the Twentieth century, July, 1937.

9. A Fragment of Mughal History, Orme,

10. The Founder of Banera, Sri Ram Sharma in Islamic culture.

11. Origins of the Rajput War of Independence, Yash Pal in I.H.Q.

12. Aurangzeb III, Jadunath Sarkar.

13. History of Mewar; Brook.

14. Biographical Sketches of the Chiefs of Mewar.

15. Chitor and the Mewar Family; Stratton.

16. Shahjahan of Delhi, B. P. Saxena.

17. Glories of Marwar, B.N. Rau.

18. Causes of the Rathor Rebellion, Mohammed Akthar Ali, Indian History Congress, 1961.

19. Indian Ephemeris, L. D. Swaminathan Pillay.

20. Chief and leading Families of Rajputana.

21 A Bibliography of medieval Rajasthan, G.N. Sharma.

Some of the original sources for the story told in the work have been reproduced in original or in English abstract in the appendices to various chapters.

INDEX